Luminescence
of the Ordinary

Luminescence
of the Ordinary

RICK HALTERMANN

Luminescence of the Ordinary. Copyright 2021 by Rick Haltermann. All rights reserved. No part of this publication may be reproduced, stored in a retrieval system, or transmitted in any form or by any means, electronic, mechanical, photocopying, recording, scanning, or otherwise, without the prior written permission of the author.

First paperback edition December 2021

Author Rick Haltermann

Cover and interior photography by Rick Haltermann

Edited by Adrienne Pond and Jocelyn Harper

Design by Kelly Pasholk, Wink Visual Arts

Published by Rick Haltermann

Print: ISBN 978-0-9907564-0-8

eBook: ISBN 978-0-9907564-1-5

Printed in the United States of America

Acknowledgements

My deepest gratitude to Jocelyn Harper for her love and penciled machete used to clear a path through the thicket of my words and thoughts. Thank you to Adrienne Pond of Lost Art Editing for her attention and timeliness. Gratitude to Kelly Pasholk of Wink Visual Arts for her graphic design in turning mere words into something to behold. And many thanks to a true brother, Tonio Epstein of The Magical Mystery Tour on WGDR, for all of the conversations and support. Finally, to you, dear reader, for being curious enough to dive in.

About The Author

Rick Haltermann's previous book was the award winning *Curriculum of the Soul*. He is also a photographer, musician, Director of the Association of Noetic Practitioners and lives in northern New Mexico.

Table of Contents

Introduction	1
Growing Into Your Loving	5
Our Sphere of Influence	9
Where Do You Put Your Attention?	13
Common Sense	17
Understanding the Landscape	21
The Loss of Civility	27
Data Deluge	31
Pause	35
The Soul	39
Other Worlds	43
Nurturing the Soul	47
A Way Forward	51
Without Initiation	55
Differences	61
The Deepening Divide	65
A Letter to the World	71
Signs	75
Deeper Currents	79
I See-Um	83
Aesthetic Considerations	87

The Fall of Jazz	91
Reading Poems Out Loud	95
A Case Against the Use of Recreational Marijuana	101
Treading the Waters of Spirituality	105
Victim Empathy	109
Moral Authority	115
Living, Not Meaning	119
My Fate	123
Training	127
The Soul's Curriculum	131
Where Do We Go From Here?	135
A Letter To A Friend	139
Mortality	145
Luminescence of the Ordinary	149
A Blessing	153
Towards a New Paradigm	155
Since The Vaccine	159
Everything Explained	163
A New Declaration of Independence	167
My Prayer	173

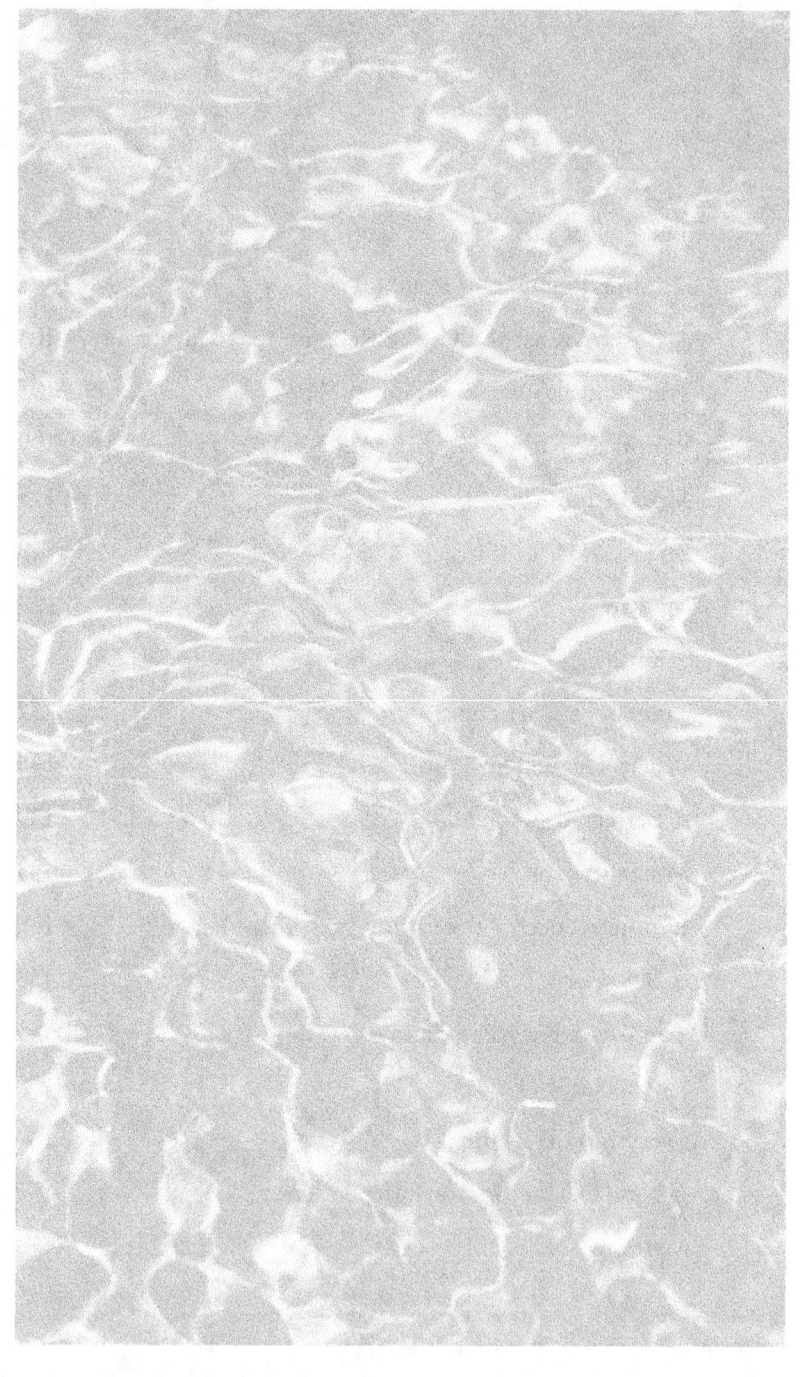

Introduction

We are filled and surrounded by infinite possibilities. Watch any young child's body in how fully inhabited it is physically and emotionally. Joy and playfulness abound with the thrill of simply being alive. Babies seem to be in a constant state of amazement whether through curiosity or hunger. Why then is it that only some adults retain this way of being while most others fall prey to preconceptions of aging and maturity? Clearly some kind of conditioning, programming or trauma has taken place.

Dominating modern culture are the literal, physical and analytical perspectives.

We live in our heads. This can be found through the pervading needs of wanting to fix our problems, needing to be attached to our identities, relying on data and searching for meaning. These views are always outward. What if we created a different relationship to those problems? Or contemplated who we really are beneath those identities? Should data always have the last word over intuition or instinct? Does the heart ever long for concepts? The literal and analytical viewpoints have created a mostly secular reality while obscuring the sacred.

Economics and politics have become the driving forces in our world. This is a boon for capitalism along with technological or scientific advancement, and, consequently, a disaster for the ecology and species of the planet. Mental (and to a much smaller extent athletic) activities are rewarded accordingly with promises of success, validation and approval. The shadow side is loneliness, anxiety, depression and other physical symptoms leading to a record number of prescription medications in this country. With the United States containing just 4.5 percent of the global population, we consume upwards to 70 percent of the worlds pharmaceuticals. In other words, we are the embodiment of modern humanity living out of harmony with how nature works.

The natural world thrives through diversity, cooperation, adaptation and knowing what's enough. My view is that modern humans need something to keep our analytical, data driven activity in check. Indigenous cultures had mythologies with spiritual dimensions that pointed to far greater knowledge and wisdom available beyond the human brain. Some call this the soul or the intermediary between the Divine and ourselves. Without getting preoccupied with semantic, religious, esoteric or philosophical views, one might generally consider this aspect of our nature as various combinations of the mental, physical, emotional, psychological and spiritual. Hence, the many possibilities mentioned above.

With the weaving of these aspects of ourselves we encounter the soul. Sadly, this is a mostly lost perspective nowadays. The old view was that the ego was here to serve the soul so that living a life would lead to "the rapture of being alive" (Joseph Campbell). Within that rapture is our loving. You can't just think your way to this place.

These essays are my attempt to remind the reader of the mysterious and oftentimes complicated world of the soul. Since writing *Curriculum of the Soul,* this has been my mission. For those of you who are not familiar, that book was, as one friend described, "everything you were never taught in school." It covered birth to death and all of the joys and challenges encountered in between, with the hope that each reader could find their own map in how to navigate being alive. As a result of creating the curriculum, my challenge has been to live up to the tenets I set forth in that book. It's not easy. All of the tools needed for being in the world and nurturing oneself are within these essays but as living examples that you might find more accessible in relationship to your own life. The map remains the same. The next step is becoming familiar with the day to day applications.

Without any predetermined outlines, I gave myself just one parameter which was to write about one thousand words per essay. I wrote as a topic arose either in my imagination or my life. Grace provided paths where I could find love within as well as beyond in the world. Hopefully, dear reader, you will discover your own luminescence of the ordinary as well.

Growing Into Your Loving

I turned sixty-five in 2017 with little fanfare as has been the case since my forties. It was October. To celebrate, I went to a hot springs spa to swim laps outdoors then read in the sun. Heaven. Aging is like a favorite piece of clothing that keeps feeling better next to the skin over time but conversely shows the wear and tear of living to the rest of the world. The main character in the film *The Great Beauty* says, "The most important thing I discovered a few days after turning sixty-five is that I can't waste any more time doing things I don't want to do." Time felt like forever while growing up with endless horizons of possibility. Now, the landscape has changed, the number of days less infinite and more precious.

About a year ago, I awoke in the middle of the night to the swirl and splash of red and blue lights coming from an ambulance in a neighbor's driveway. The lights lasted for almost two hours leaving a sudden blur of seriousness. The next day over the phone, the neighbor almost matter-of-factly told me that his wife had died due to an enlarged heart that could no longer go on. I took the matter-of-factness to be an indication of shock. They had thought it was just the flu. She and I had worked together on a board for one year so we spoke almost daily during that time. Due to this one interrupted night, there's now an empty space where I once held on to a friendship. The poet Stanley Kunitz posed a question in his poem "The Layers" that I keep repeating to myself: "How shall the heart be reconciled/ to its feast of losses?"

The only time I ever got to say goodbye to someone knowing it would be the last was with my father as he lay in a coma in his eighty-ninth year. We had a fraught relationship as I grew up. Years ago, I started to do serious inner work through reading and therapy. Seeing my parents for the first time as flawed human beings, like the rest of us, was my initiation into true adulthood. As the Buddha once allegedly said, "To understand everything is to forgive everything." Will I ever fully understand my parents and their own childhoods, both living through the Great Depression and World War II and later raising a family of four children without any of the psychological and communication tools now available? Probably not, but I can try. This partial understanding is what changed my relationship with my father so that we could speak openly and with caring during the later years of his life. It was from this place that I visited him for the last time. My family has never been dramatic under any circumstances so I was not prepared for the tsunami of sensations taking place. Like an unexpected blessing, a well of feeling erupted that crystallized into gratitude, regardless of history, for my very breath and the gift of life given to me by my mother and father. I kissed my father on his forehead, said goodbye, and walked outside as I drowned in my own feelings. My world would never be the same.

About every other month, I have play dates with a dear friend. Ada was then five. She sent me a Christmas card where she wrote "Ricky Roo, I love you" a couple of times as practice with her new handwriting. When we are together, we *really* play. This isn't about supervision but about simply having close to unbridled fun with someone who is yet to be encumbered with cultural beliefs, the indoctrination of education and the heartache of suffering. To be reminded through this playing of the joy of unconditional love is one of the great pleasures of being alive, a way to compensate for the loss of my father and friends.

It's Christmas Eve, a wonderful time for reflection. Here's a list of some of my favorite things in no particular order: nature, dogeared books, the scent of sage after a summer rain, immersion in the silky texture of water, children playing, the incredible softness of my young son's hair resting against my skin as he slept, anything baked from scratch, Bill Evan's version of "My Foolish Heart," the barn raising scene in the film *Witness*, African dance, guitar playing, fireworks, Thai food, open roads, the salt flats during low tide on Cape Cod Bay in September, conversations with my mother (age 96) every week by phone, my sister's easy laugh, the early morning and late afternoon light in the Southwest, the sound of a kora, ho'oponopono, Albert King singing "As The Years Go Passing By," cold nights with flannel sheets, the smell of plumeria and gardenia and jasmine, the miracle of touch, a kiss on the back of the neck, my dreams, a kind word, belly laughing and the poet Jane Kenyon's gorgeous line: "and God, as promised, proves / to be mercy clothed in light" ("Notes From The

Other Side").

These connections within ourselves and with others create the fabric of our lives. With the joy of discovering and loving who you are comes the work of discerning what gets in the way of that loving and figuring out how not to "waste any more time doing things I (you) don't want to do." Then there is the joy of loving what you do. This is your art which encompasses *any* creative endeavor. Sometimes I wonder if being human is just about whether one is in their loving or not. And since we all fall out of that loving, what do we do to return? That may be the real work. Even at my age, I'm still looking for clues to help with the tools I've already learned.

Our Sphere of Influence

I still believe in the handmade world. I don't own a smartphone and only use a flip phone while traveling. I have no subscriptions to television, streaming or otherwise. I never have the feeling that I'm missing something in the current zeitgeist. My news comes through the radio and online where I can scroll down a page to see where there might be something uplifting. As Paul Simon sang, "I can gather all the news I need on the weather report."

While growing up in the Hudson Valley, there were just a handful of news outlets: three network television stations, a local newspaper, a local radio station and The New York Times. Only so much information could pass through these six outlets. Now it's a cornucopia of news from hundreds of sources. Today's news alone included flooding in California with casualties, ongoing war in the Middle East, record temperatures in Australia and the good news that North and South Korea are speaking to each other once again. I'll be honest; there's just too much information for my emotional body to take in, much less handle. How does one find relief?

My parents met and fell in love through ballroom dancing. This was the time of big band music when everyone moved to the sounds of jazz. Their love of dance may have been the seed for my own life. A community of friends was created through waltz, cha-cha, fox trot and swing. A world based on joy. I don't know if I ever saw my parents happier. I used to teach African dance because I love the form and the energy that emanates from live drumming. Because Africans have never been hung up about perfect poise, the possibilities for delight are endless. People always remark about how I'm usually smiling when I dance. I'm never conscious of the fact but a smile is always infectious. To paraphrase the poet Gregory Orr, if the Divine didn't want us to move, then why all this music?

I help coordinate a small organization which is involved with a new healing modality. One member had been complaining about the obsolescence of using "snail mail" to send checks to pay dues. He calls this old way of doing things "the dark ages." I explained to him recently that I know all of my postal workers on a first-name basis. Through these relationships, I also know about their aches and pains which gives me the opportunity to use the Hawaiian practice of ho'oponopono and to practice kindness. Spirituality through connection.

One of the great pleasures of the post office is the world of stamps that was taught to me by my grandfather. He used to collect whole sheets whenever a new stamp was released in the 1930s and 1940s. I still love the artwork, the histories and the imagination involved. Where else can one find beautiful art put to use on something as functional as paying a bill? Lately, I've been buying the stamps with "Love" spelled as skywriting and have been thinking about those stamps in the same way that Emoto Masaru used words like "love" and "peace" placed on a container of water to impact the structure of that water.

Beyond the stamps and the relationships at my post office, I can go one step further by mailing cards I've created with my photographs. Yes, I'll still write notes by hand to a ninety-five-year-old friend who is not interested in owning a computer or using email. In a sense, we get to touch each other's lives in a palpable way. My mother still sends me a note every week in her print style of correspondence. What a wonder it is to be able to walk in my mother's words. A few years ago, I received a card from a woman with exquisite script writing. I've kept that card as a memory of a time when civility equalled that quality of that kind of penmanship. Does anyone write love letters anymore?

I'm not averse to technology at all. But I think that discernment needs to be used when it comes to all of the electronic tools at our disposal. I post my photos of nature on Facebook to remind my friends of a world that is much larger than politics, economics, disaster and celebrity. For me, the shot of a beautiful landscape, sunset or flower is like using a pause button on our busy lives. To my elderly friends, this window helps them to keep in touch with places that are no longer physically accessible. Nature is a wonderful antidote if you might be addicted to technology.

The handmade world isn't interested in outcomes as much as slowing down to savor the moment. This mirrors the natural world which moves to its own rhythm regardless of technology. These worlds share their beauty without reservation. What are you doing to share your gifts with the world? The opportunities are unlimited. Through those gifts, a sphere of influence is created that impacts more than any of us can ever know. Even if we can't see immediate results, seeds are being planted all of the time. I have great faith in those seeds and their potential to blossom into spheres of connection, blooms of loving.

Where Do You Put Your Attention?

We live in a time where our culture demands our attention, through catastrophic news, politics, economics, social media and entertainment. This has been amplified through the use of computers and smartphones. Since much of this information is external, the negative impact from this barrage on our individual inner lives has been profound. More than ever, sanity requires a healthy sense of discernment so that one doesn't become overwhelmed. How many people do you know who answer the question, "How are you?" with anything other than "Fine," "Good," "OK," "Busy," "Stressed," or "Exhausted"?

"(A)nd no one says *How aren't you?*" (Rumi, *Say Yes Quickly*)

This information deluge is due not only to the connectivity of our devices but also to the larger fact that many of the older paradigms are changing drastically within our lifetimes. This includes institutions like government, marriage, religion, the workplace and education. Even gender identity and the climate are in flux. Without a center to hold things together, it is a wild time to be alive. Since the cultural, political and social structures are no longer what they used to be, more and more pressure is placed upon the individual to take some form of personal responsibility. As these institutions falter, our tendencies are to fixate—like watching a building in the moment of demolition. It's hard to look away. But the change is taking place over a period of time, rather than a moment. Refocusing might be healthier than entrancement.

A woman I know was intent on finding every negative news article online about President Trump. As a result, all she did was complain about his actions. One day I suggested a news diet. Criticizing politicians is like shooting fish in a barrel. I'm baffled by the thought that politics could have precedence over one's inner life. Perhaps this accounts for the lack of smiles I see publicly. Could events in Washington, D.C. really be more important than one's own happiness? Is it possible that well-being could be determined by the actions taking place elsewhere? It's as though our culture has been reduced to watching everything as if it is a sporting event. If your side wins, a good mood is guaranteed.

What's the alternative? I've chosen a healthy lifestyle that insists on self-care over being distracted. Needless to say, discernment has become essential in determining everything from diet to friends. Oftentimes I'll consider the energetics of these influences to make sure they support my well-being. This includes the necessity of spending time in and exercising in nature on a regular basis. I can walk in fields of sage directly from my home or take a short drive to be on alpine trails that parallel streams in the high country. There is always the quiet news of witnessing the seasons change, watching flowers blossoming then going to seed, and knowing that fresh air is precious.

Years ago, I was a property manager in Vail, Colorado. One January morning, I woke up with such pain in my lower back that I had to crawl on all fours just to get to the bathroom. It turned out that my sacroiliac joint (SI) was out of place. I went to a chiropractor who adjusted me but also suggested that I eliminate refined sugar, coffee (caffeine) and processed flour from my diet which would take some stress off the adrenal glands that control the SI joint. I took his advice and it worked! That was the beginning of a new diet which has slowly become all organic. I'm now astonished when going into a regular grocery store and seeing how much food is processed or altered by genetic engineering. Common sense tells me that our bodies are much happier eating real food.

I love swimming laps, hiking, skiing, snowshoeing and dancing to live music frequently. Dancing is about fun and seeing how my body responds to the music. Being in the water or on the trail is similar to a meditation which I also do every morning on a couch just after waking up. This is just what works for me. I find great joy in reading or watching a film. When going out, it's either to connect with a friend to enjoy their company at an art event like theater, live music or a poetry reading.

Beneath all of this is trying to stay present and seeing where I am moment to moment in terms of kindness, humor, compassion, patience and surrender. Rather than the news of the external world as a preoccupation, the real news, for me, is the state of my inner world that may or may not create some sort of grace. The events of our lives are always giving us feedback. Grace is feeling a sense of flow and love in any moment. Being out of grace is when things aren't working.

I once had a client with high sensibilities, perhaps psychic, who claimed that he couldn't walk into a grocery store without hearing the thoughts of everyone around him. Initially, my wonder was aroused in terms of how hard that must be. A friend has said that when going into a bar he can feel people cleaning their energy off on him; like he's some kind of sponge with no protection due to over absorption. Over time, I've come to realize that both men have very poor boundaries and a lack of respect for others' privacy. Underneath, there's probably some narcissism taking place that uses their sensitivities to draw attention towards themselves. The soul cops would have them arrested for such misplaced attention.

Joseph Campbell talks about "the rapture of being alive" when the experiences on the physical plane resonate with the deepest part of who we are. As I discover more and more of that deep place, I try to be aware if it is influencing on my outer world. Yes, things do keep getting better when I align with and cultivate what resonates for me. It has simply become a practice of focus.

Common Sense

On January 10, 1776, Thomas Paine published *Common Sense* which contained a series of arguments in favor of independence for the Thirteen American Colonies from Great Britain. As of 2006, it remains the all-time best selling American title, and is still in print today. Not only does this speak to the power of reason, but to the power of reasoning that was made accessible and palatable while speaking to the immediate moment. Here is one of my favorite quotes from the pamphlet: "I draw my idea of the form of government from a principle in nature, which no art can overturn, viz. that the more simple any thing is, the less liable it is to be disordered, and the easier repaired when disordered."

The folk wisdom version of common sense relied on this simplicity mentioned above. Keeping it simple *had* to be learned from nature if one was to survive. This depended on self-reliance so that the efficient splitting of wood, for instance, meant a warm home. I used to live in Vermont where they say that firewood heats you twice: once while you split and once when it burns. And if you've ever experienced a chimney fire, you'll either learn to clean a fireplace yourself or hire someone else on a regular basis. The alternative can be a lost home.

Due to drought and the resulting forest wildfires in the American West, building a wooden structure in the midst of a forest without any defensible space around it has resulted in the loss of thousands of homes. In Colorado, I once purchased a piece of property that overlooked Mt. Sopris in the Roaring Fork Valley. The view was spectacular while the land was covered with cedar and pine. This was within a homeowner's association that did not allow for the removal of trees. So I proposed building a straw-bale home due to the fire-resistant properties. Compressed straw doesn't breathe, so, without air, fire can't happen. Simple. The association insisted on wooden structures. When I asked the property manager what would happen in the event of an inferno, he said, "Grab your keys, get in the car and go." I sold the property.

So what has happened to common sense? In general, our relationship with nature has diminished in favor of the vibrancy of urban areas. Several years ago, a very wet spring took place where I live. It was raining almost every day which is unusual for northern New Mexico. I hike often and am usually prepared for changing weather. Out I went on a trail that initially parallels a stream then heads up to a peak about four miles further. In less than a mile, it began to rain then, hail. I stood underneath a favorite pine tree which offered good protection while I put on my rain gear and waited. The hail turned back into rain. I became concerned when that hail buried all of the new ground cover. I'd never seen that before. Then the trail itself turned into a raging little creek. This didn't look good. I made a quick decision to return to my car and started jogging back down the trail. In the thirty or so minutes I had been waiting, the stream had risen four or five inches so that the rocks initially used to cross were now underwater. I ran straight through. When I made it safely down and took off my Gore-Tex boots, there were about four ounces of water in each. Another hiker visiting from Atlanta wasn't so lucky that day. He had gone out wearing a windbreaker and sneakers and climbed to the peak. They found his body in the stream a week later about a mile up from where I had turned back. Heartbreaking. Wanting to look at a vista is very different from being in touch with a changing landscape in order to make good decisions.

I recently read about an app that reminds the user when to drink water and in what quantity. The author of the article discovered the app after her body had been breaking down and her doctor asked about how much water she drank every day. The answer was next to none. What does it say when we've gotten to the point where our smartphones are given more power than our own physical ability to sense? Technology, as wonderful as it is, can't replace what it *feels* like to be alive.

My fear is that since our culture has moved more into urban areas, our electronic devices have become the first source for information rather than such important tools as our bodies, instincts and intuitions. This is playing out through increased child accidents on playgrounds as parents are distracted with their electronic devices. Pedestrians are now losing their lives by walking in front of moving vehicles because they are too focused on their handheld screens. Drivers themselves are causing one in four accidents due to being distracted by cell phone use. Accidents and harm to humans indicate that new technologies might need some balancing within the wider arc of our attention.

I met a man yesterday who told me about a chameleon type of characteristic that he has learned. When traveling to unfamiliar places, he pays attention to the way people dress, their unique use of language, what they eat and how they act. A little curiosity and humility go a long way. Through this method, he can begin to immerse himself into a new culture as he goes about his own business. As Ralph Waldo Emerson once said, "Common sense is genius dressed in its working clothes."

Understanding the Landscape

The place where I am from is in the Hudson Valley of New York State. I was wedged between three siblings, the river and the Catskills. This was before Pete Seegar's *Clearwater* sloop project raised awareness about pollution in the Hudson so the river was rarely a destination. Instead, the nooks and crannies of those mountains held everything from exploring the Woodstock Playhouse to hiking up Slide Mountain to learning to ski via rope tow in Phoenicia to driving back roads that followed streams like tendrils off of Route 28. Beyond the Colonial clapboard house where I grew up, this was home.

This was also before the Internet and electronic devises. My free time as a youth was usually spent outdoors exploring the woods, playing by a stream, chasing summer fireflies and planting gardens. Winter was the time to make some extra money shoveling sidewalks in the neighborhood, to sled down Linderman Avenue and to ski in the mountains. My father would drive us to Cape Cod each summer to spend up to a month on the bay side, in a small cabin. We spent whole days at the beach as the tide receded and returned determining where we could and couldn't play. The Catskills and the beaches of the Atlantic Ocean became my templates for where I was most comfortable. Doesn't everyone have their own personal terrain?

When I speak of the landscape, there is a mystery that rises out of the land, or water, itself. It could be the smell of roses in a garden, the soft light found at the edges of the day or deer grazing in a field. Older cultures were the result of this *intimacy* with the environment created through topography, climate, vegetation, the possibility for shelter and the availability of food. This rapport, which governed survival and the sustainability of their cultures, is what allowed Indigenous people to sometimes thrive or oftentimes perish if conditions changed drastically. There is still no finding for the disappearance of the Anasazi in the Southwest. About one hundred thousand bushmen are all that are left, roaming the plains of the Kalahari desert in Africa. Aboriginal population in Australia is presumed to have fallen from the millions to less than seven hundred thousand today. My fear is that an essential *knowing* is being lost in favor of technology, our primary source for modern knowledge.

In Bruce Chatwin's book, *The Songlines*, he puts forth a theory about Aboriginal culture during the period predating humans known as the "Dreamtime", the theory being that original ancestors *sang* the birds, the rocks, the streams, the vegetation and the terrain into existence. This was the beginning of the Aborigine language. Each particular landscape then represented a song that had been memorized by a particular clan (snake, kangaroo, bird, for example) who, at one time, walked the path of the "songline" each year as a pilgrimage in honor of the ancestors of the Dreamtime. It is hard to fathom that kind of intimacy with the landscape anymore.

For the Aborigine, the knowledge of the terrain extended well beyond survival. It became the poetry of song. Imagine knowing a place so well that the relationship becomes a kind of love that calls on us to take a level of responsibility towards the well-being of that ground. Cherishing nature insists upon preserving that which one loves. This is what Edward Abbey was writing about in his books dealing with the Southwest. He pointed out that once the ruins and artifacts now under Lake Powell are submerged, for instance, they can never be restored. The fields and woods near where I grew up have all been developed and turned into housing. Is there any place that exists as we once knew it? If not, what does that do to our sense of being in the world today?

Due to the spreading of populations, by boat, train and air, the question now has become more global than local. What will it take, if it is even possible, to understand this larger perspective? Since Western culture values and rewards mental activity far more than sensuousness, the places we loved may become lost like the almost 150-200 species of plants, animals and insects that are going extinct every day. Perhaps we are being called upon to create our own threads and "songlines" locally as a foundation for the larger work. Simone Weil wrote, "To be rooted is perhaps the most important and least recognized need of the human soul." Being *with* the landscape is very different than just visiting.

At the moment, about 80 percent of the U.S. population

relies on a smartphone. That technology can help one understand where they are physically and perhaps culturally if there is reception. But how do we understand where we are in the outer world on a deeper more intimate level—emotionally, psychologically and aesthetically? Using an intermediary device can get in the way of direct feeling and knowing with our senses. That device can also create an arrogance combined with ignorance when it comes to local customs.

Every Christmas Eve at Taos Pueblo in New Mexico, the Procession of the Virgin Mary takes place at sunset followed by the burning of multiple bonfires in the plaza area. Photography is not permitted at the Pueblo with ample signage to remind the visitor. This has always been the case. I was astonished recently during this holiday with how many visitors were using their smartphones to photograph the event. Simply being there and respecting the wishes of the hosts are apparently no longer enough.

I'm not trying to romanticize the Indigenous relationship to the landscape. What I am lamenting is the loss of the intimacy that was required to have this relationship. That loss represents a diminishment of our feeling function and hence our connection to the planet. Technology, by nature, can only move forward. Even in the last ten years the advancements have been remarkable. Whole social, political and humanitarian movements have taken place thanks to social media. In turn, I've been looking for evidence of the benefits of modern technology on a personal level beyond speed and efficiency. Have those values surpassed the human values of caring and connection to the landscape and to one another?

I now live in the desert where the Native Tiwa People and Hispanics have lived for centuries. There is a humility required to live here due to the established traditions of those who were here first and because the desert is as unforgiving as it is spectacular. The general attitude is unpretentious and self-sufficient. I'm still wedged between the the mountains and the river. But there is something about all of the open space in the West that allows for an emotional freedom I couldn't experience back east. Perhaps I'm escaping from my past and maybe I'm just beginning to understand myself well enough so I can love and be a part of this new landscape as it extends to the future.

The Loss of Civility

Civility is a standard agreed upon by a society on how others will be treated: basically, as you would want to be treated yourself. It began as an understanding between individuals then expanded into the community and country. Of course, there have always been those—criminals, perpetuators of domestic violence, and people who don't keep their word, for example—who break the social contract. Yet they stand out strikingly against the larger backdrop of fairness and decency. For my parents, civility included the integrity of good conduct, honesty and mutual respect. In other words, it was the aspiration towards the seven virtues: chastity, temperance, charity, diligence, patience, kindness and humility. Good manners were also involved along with courtesies such as always responding to an invitation, sending a thank you note or naturally being polite. The shadow side was an adherence to convention and norms which encouraged conformity regardless of circumstance. Whether that conformity was in an abusive relationship or within the unique problems of addiction, it was swept under the rug, not to be discussed in polite company. In the 1950s and early 1960s, it was a taboo to divorce, thus holding the family structure intact.

As the world's population keeps increasing, we are seen less as individuals and more as members of a group. This can be a problem. Our culture is clumsy when it comes to identifying and defining people within these larger, unknown groups that pop up with such frequency these days. They include gender, race, marital status, age, migrants, health and political preference among many others. If one doesn't fit a certain prescribed demographic, it can be more difficult to be seen or regarded. Beyond groups, individuals are now mostly recognized through the lens of celebrity, success or as a victim of some disaster. Many other new, different voices want to be heard. This may explain the current popularity of memoir writing to tell our own stories within the greater and sometimes overwhelming currents of our time. As we become lost in the masses, a desperate need arises for the individual to be seen.

The number of humans today on the planet is now three times what it was when my parents married in 1948. Since 2008, more people live in cites than not. With urban life comes congestion, pollution (air, noise and light) and traffic that usually surpasses the capacity of the inadequate infrastructure. Even with the social, economic, intellectual, cultural and recreational advantages, new research shows that stress is on the rise. When one includes this with the creation of the Internet and its offspring, social media, the combination of stress and anonymity via technology is a perfect petri dish for individual expression of that stress. Anger, rage and even hate fill the Internet and spill into our twenty-four-hour news diets. Words that would never be considered fifty years ago are now commonplace. Instead of civility, verbal aggression has erupted. Hostile assertiveness has evolved as well, which materializes in public bombings, school shootings, increased domestic violence and, to a less horrific extent but still alarming, politics.

What were the watershed moments? For me, the murders of John F. Kennedy and Martin Luther King, Jr.; the discovery through the Pentagon Papers that our government was capable of lying, thus costing thousands of lives; the tactics used by the Nixon re-election campaign to justify character assassination along with indifference to constitutional law; the Columbine High School killings and the 9/11 attacks.

The boundaries for decency keep being violated. The killing of prominent people is not new and politics has always had a dark and dirty side. However, it keeps getting dirtier and polarized by the identities of left versus right, or Republican versus Democrat so that actual discourse in Washington, D.C. is now rare. One of many disturbing aspects of the school shootings is that we can no longer be assured of our children's safety while they are learning (and out of our sight). September 11th reinforced this idea that the inviolability of public places was and is no longer guaranteed.

These tragic events seem to have created a new precedent on a personal level as well. Perhaps this is a consequence of increasing distrust in government specifically and loss of faith in authority in general. What happened to holding a door open for someone, to being on time, to giving a pregnant woman a seat on public transportation, to ending a relationship face to face rather than by texting, to giving two weeks' notice when leaving a job, to saying, "I'm sorry" or "Thank you" when the opportunity arises, to having eye contact with another person to asking, "Excuse me, am I interrupting your conversation"? Being civil was once the glue of civilization. Without that glue, what have we become?

There are other things that have disabled courtesy over the past thirty years which are equally disturbing. In politics, inventing stories about an opponent regardless of fact is the new standard. Misinformation abounded and Donald Trump created over thirty thousand false claims during his four years in office. This is the result of the older trend from the 1980s where anyone was willing to tell you what you wanted to hear rather than being honest. I discovered this by working with general contractors in Colorado; I often heard "yes" to any potential work even though the person had no intention or skills to fulfill the requests. Now it is commonplace to hear about unscrupulous contractors and car mechanics who will charge whatever they can get away with—especially with women.

With the loss of civility comes a reminder of a loss of common courtesy in America. Here is where I grieve. Graciousness seems to have been replaced with cynicism, bullying and a lengthening of the distance to truth. This plays out with so many factions today who are opposed to each other. Civility might begin anew with making, at minimum, verbal amends to Native and African Americans. To the soldiers who fought in the Vietnam War and wars since. To the families who lost members in those wars. To women for unequal pay, sexual harassment and violence. To any person of color who has been mistreated simply because they weren't born in America. Finally, to our children for our inability to pass on the full promise, respect and care of this land. By example, those amends could help foster a new caring that reimagines a civility based on the tender fragility we all share as humans.

Data Deluge

Lately, the first and last word has been left up to data, research or "experts." The rallying cry of the challenger in an argument or discussion is now "show me the science" (if they even still believe in facts). It is no coincidence that this trend has appeared with the advent of the Internet, computers, smartphones and apps. These are the new Gods of our culture that give us information immediately and with instant gratification. What an amazing time to be alive. I can Google the number of deaths due to the Crusades (1.7 million), use Wikipedia to find out the meaning and origin of the term "anima mundi" (Latin, world soul) or look up the weather of a destination when traveling (please, no thunderstorms near the airport). All of this can be done in less than a minute.

A friend recently forwarded an article titled, "One-third of Americans can't eat without their cellphones, study finds." The research goes on to say that 72 percent watch television while eating. Those people found this activity more pleasurable than talking to their friends or family. As an unintended consequence, food is consumed so quickly that portion size is rarely considered for 57 percent of those surveyed. What lies under these statistics? There is addiction, loneliness, lack of human connection and interaction along with the false belief that being busy is somehow equivalent to being productive.

How have we come to give an electronic device so much power over our lives? Is this a reflection of the crumbling faith in the power of our religious institutions? Has data become the new commandment in directing or controlling how we live? Yes, I have a desktop iMac along with a flip phone that I use while traveling. My cell phone will never compete with the clarity of my landline. If I had a preference, it would be spending time outdoors and in nature over being in front of a screen. For me, the technological world provides a wonderful means for information, entertainment and creativity, not an altar I have to bow down to.

Without going into too much detail, here is what recent studies report about smartphone and cellphone use (Yes, I admit to using the Internet to find this data.): currently, 95 percent of adult Americans now own cell phones while 77 percent own smartphones. Out of one thousand university students studied in ten countries, most could not go twenty-four hours without using their devices. Like with any addiction, withdrawal is painful. Due to mobile phone use, there has been an increase in back problems, anxiety and depression, stress, alienation and weight management issues. These coincide with decreased fitness, disrupted sleep, loss of attention span, eyesight damage, possible effects from radiation, child accidents due to distracted adults, pedestrian deaths due to autos (up 11 percent between 2016 and 2017), car accidents (up 52 percent in 2016) and motor vehicle deaths (for a total of 3,477 in 2015). Fewer people are out in the wilderness perhaps due to the lack of phone reception available.

An addiction is when we no longer have control over the use of something (drugs, alcohol, food, sex and technology, for instance) even in the face of resulting adverse consequences. What harm can there be in the cultural belief that more, in this case, information is better? The casualties are what lie deep within: silence and solitude as tools to keep in touch with oneself. With their loss comes the diminishment of intuition and possibly instinct. In turn, discernment and discipline, in conjunction with any addiction, are forgotten. Then there is the loss of human contact and connection. What does it say when a relationship to an object is preferred over that with a human? One certainty from all of this is that we as a culture are far more in our heads than our bodies.

What's to be done? As with any addiction, nothing can change until the toxicity is acknowledged and fully confronted. Our culture still has a prevailing belief in profits over peril. In America, change sometimes happens only after enough people are harmed or even die. Examples are Ralph Nader's crusade against the Chevrolet Corvair, the tobacco industry's cover up of the relationship between smoking and lung cancer, the mining industry's denial of black lung disease and Exxon's hidden research since 1977 regarding the effects of carbon emissions on the climate. The thought that lives can be altered for the worse and are expendable for the sake of industry is chilling.

The tradeoff seems to be that speed and efficiency of obtaining facts, texts, emails and postings is now a priority over the information given by our bodies through sensory awareness, physical symptoms, dreams, and our gut reactions. This is illustrated by the United States's dominance in consuming up to 70 percent of the world's pharmaceutical medications—particularly anti-depressants. It's far more expedient to eliminate the symptom than to have to waste all of that effort rooting out and working on the cause. One in six Americans are now on these meds. This may represent our mechanical view of the physical body that can be used, abused and fixed if necessary.

The potential distraction of data through gadgets is like a spell cast upon the user. If you were born in the past thirty years, chances are your world is tied inextricably with technological devices. Add the contemporary belief regarding the importance of being relevant and what choice does a young person have? I remember when my son was around nine-years-old and just discovering games on the computer. Watching him one afternoon, I suggested doing something different. He replied, "But Rick, I'm addicted." I couldn't argue with that. Instead, I set a new boundary that every minute in front of the screen would require an equal amount of time outdoors. Twenty years later, he still likes to play computer games. The difference now is that they seem to have lost much of their charm.

Pause

I love good radio as much as being engrossed in a good book. Time disappears, the tea simmers and my imagination is left to roam a landscape that is not determined by a fixed image or constant commercial interruption. Fifty years ago, I began as a DJ at St. Lawrence University when I was a sophomore. The school is the home of North Country Public Radio, WSLU, which is a professional station. We students operated entry level KSLU which, at the time, broadcast through the telephone lines of the dormitories. Out of approximately two thousand potential student listeners, it would be safe to say that it was only our friends who tuned in. The only exception was when co-hosting a show with a Deadhead who insisted on playing "Dark Star" behind the top of the hour newscast. Who would have thought that the station manager would tune in that very morning?

In all of those years since, I've played jazz then added poetry during special occasions like Valentine's Day. Now it's jazz and poetry combined with weekly themes. The themes might be the music of an artist, a particular poet or a holiday. Usually I'm looking for something less obvious but with a strong enough thread to connect to an audience. I tend not to play mainstream jazz since it is exhaustively broadcast on public radio. Instead, melody, texture and the feel of the music is the focus. It's currently a Sunday morning show which, for me, requires a bit of calm and reverence. A woman called me once to say how much she hated jazz but loved what I was doing. After over nine hundred shows at my current station, KTAO, coming up with a new theme with new poems can be challenging. This past week as I was getting ready for bed, I asked my dreams for an idea. A few hours later, I woke up and an internal voice quietly said, "Try a little tenderness." Oh my soul...

Thanks to the feedback from a couple of friends, something occurred to me that I hadn't considered before. The show has become kind of a pause button for the listener; a moment when the noise and events of the world can be put on hold perhaps long enough to take a break and recharge. This result has been accidental but, I now understand, more needed than ever. Between smartphones and the Internet, there is perhaps too much information at our fingertips which can have an addictive quality. How long can you go without using your phone or computer? For me, my desktop device is used about once a day for reading the news, communicating, editing photographs, finding poems for a radio show and writing.

There is a story about a man in a Detroit suburb who was considering committing suicide by jumping off an overpass into oncoming traffic. It was 1:00 a.m. The police closed the road and asked the semi-truck drivers who were waiting anyway if they might create a safety net by parking below the bridge so that the man's fall would not be life threatening. For three hours, thirteen trucks parked side by side filling the width of the six-lane highway. The man eventually came down and was taken to a hospital for counseling. All of those truck drivers needed to be elsewhere yet they choose to do good while forced to pause for the sake of helping a stranger who was at risk.

I often going hiking or snowshoeing at least once a week in an alpine environment where trails loosely parallel and repeatedly cross streams. The sound of water is a constant companion. That moisture is what nourishes heart-leafed arnica, cow parsnip, mountain ash, monkshood, yellow coneflower, wild strawberries and raspberries, ferns, horsetail and Indian pipe. If I'm attentive and lucky, I also see lady slippers (Calypso orchids). The trails slowly work their way uphill to a ridge where numerous springs begin the flow of water. There is a large grove of aspens about a mile up one and it is like walking into the majesty of a cathedral. During high fall, the combination of spotted off-white aspen tree trunks, flaming gold leaves and the brilliant blue of the western sky is enough to say that it would be a good day to die. Or at least rest for awhile and try to take it all in.

While taking photographs on one of those autumn days in that very grove, another photographer was there with lots of equipment and lenses having the time of his life as nature wore her brightest clothes. We spoke about the colors and the light. He asked if I came there often. I told him that I was on that trail year-round and it was never the same even after just a few days apart. Weather changes, plants grow to blossom then go to seed, trees fall as a new crop of aspens fills in the grove and I never know how I'm going to feel on any given day. There are a lot of variables yet being immersed in the rhythm, sounds and sights of nature is like a salve to my soul when the human world has become overwhelming. A sweet sadness emerges when it's time for me to head back down to my car, and return to the man-made world.

The bushmen of the Kalahari Desert are said to need about sixteen hours a week for survival-specific activities. The rest is free time. Since they own only what they can carry, the burden of property is not a problem. There is nothing romantic about a survivalist lifestyle. But I wonder if pausing is ever needed since they are fully tuned into the rhythm of the earth. Indigenous cultures everywhere know this. But as modern culture grows further and further away from that rhythm, we've created everything from apps to retreats to vacations to meds to try to return to the natural pace of our bodies.

If I'm not in the woods, at least I'm outdoors. Come join me.

The Soul

Depending on your background, whether it be religious, philosophical, scientific or spiritual, descriptions of the soul are as varied as wildflowers in a meadow. If you have no specific belief (or belief systems), the soul is simply a mystery or enigma. In general, the word is used very loosely in contemporary culture usually to describe a depth of feeling. "It touched me to my soul." Anyone can now make a pronouncement and get away with it since no consensual understanding exists. This is distressing without the bearings of a shared agreement of what the concept means. Losing sight of this concept has been like having no lighthouse to help guide us through the rough seas, shoals and rocks of the waters of life.

 The Irish poet, theologian and philosopher, John O'Donahue, spoke of the soul as "a shy, intimate, subtle presence" preferring the nuance of shadows to "the language of analysis [that] has a false light in it—a kind of neon light that is too harsh for the subtlety of the soul." This idea alone presents the place where we have fully embraced rationality by taking the road well-traveled looking outward for answers rather than inward for hints, signs and wisdom. Knowledge is just information but *can* become wisdom through the help of experience and the knowing light of your soul.

With our increasing use of technology, we have created Gods out of data, science and rational thinking. This carries the curse of the belief that we can fix anything with enough studies, research and funding. But what about an intimate relationship that may need to go through its twists and turns to find another place for growth? Or sitting with the ambiguity of a dream so that it may reveal itself over time? Or wondering about the roots of my own dissatisfactions and whether I'm willing to do anything about them?

I embrace the idea of an essence of who we are as humans apart from our identity. This essence, the soul, is the foundation of what enlivens us through love. So if a notion like racism or misogyny doesn't come from our loving, what part of us is it connected to? All of the things that create identity, by definition, have to do with the ego. When approval, validation, acceptance or notoriety appear (basically thoughts about oneself), you know the ego is involved. This isn't bad per se—it's just not the place of the soul whose identity has never been a concern. What the ego and soul both share is the need for a body as a way to experience being alive.

As much as the soul doesn't care for lists, rules or clocks (the linear mind in action), there are some distinctions that can be made. Our ego-centered world is obsessed with identity through material success, happiness via consumption, politics, economics, celebrity and catastrophe. These all parallel technological growth which has resulted in keeping us in our heads without integrating our body and its corresponding sensations, feelings, intuition and gut knowing. The trade-off is the possible loss of our connection to the subtle body and thus the soul. Unlike rational thought, the soul shows up as a consequence, accidentally and without warning, if it shows up at all. For instance, conversation might be a path to connection. Helping someone could open the door to compassion. Good humor usually brings forth play and joy. Surrounding yourself with the beauty of nature or art is a diet that often nurtures the soul. It is not the physical act alone but in the weaving of the physical, emotional, psychological and spiritual that the connection to the soul can take place.

The access to the soul is found through the extent to which we can be present and attentive with our awareness in noticing the connection between our inner and outer worlds. In the film *Lady Bird,* the nun in charge of the school says, "Aren't those the same? Love and attention?" This is what the soul yearns for; for us to pay attention instead of constantly being distracted. We love to the extent we can focus. Consider the instant access to news, information, entertainment and communication alone. Our presence is continually being fractured by the connection to these possibilities. Mindfulness retreats have become a sort of antidote but have you noticed any real affects culturally? What I have noticed is how easily the ego can be manipulated through social media and technological joyrides. The Buddhists have been talking for ages about how effortlessly the mind can be distracted. So all of this is nothing new.

For me, the deeper question has to do with what we are losing in terms of silence, solitude, intuition and, hence, access to our innate wisdom found in the soul. Soul time prefers slow time which is not necessarily efficient. This is the rhythm of the earth. Wherever the seeds of our souls come from, there is a lifelong process of growing into this astonishing aspect of ourselves. In other words, with the natural human tendency to create and rely on identity, some self-reflection and transformation is required to reveal the quiet underpinnings of the soul. Its evolution may be the real reason why we are here on Earth.

I believe that each soul has its own curriculum; it creates both positive and negative patterns in our lives so we can exercise our free will and, hopefully, learn accordingly. The soul has a kind of neutrality which makes no distinction between illness, joy or the blues. It gives us choices that lead either towards or away from love and arranges the pieces of our lives—good, bad or ugly—so that we might realize who we are without the burden and illusion of ego identity. Rather than identity, it's all just experience and information to guide us through grace into the arms of love. To quote Rumi,

> *Out beyond ideas*
> *of wrongdoing and rightdoing,*
> *there is a field.*
>
> *I'll meet you there.*
>
> *When the soul lies down*
> *in that grass,*
> *the world is too full to talk about.*
>
> *Ideas, language*
> *—even the phrase "each other"—*
> *doesn't make any sense.*

Other Worlds

My car mechanic recently told me a story about a man who worked at the Saab factory in Sweden. That man's job was putting tires on the left side of the cars at the very end of the assembly process. After years of doing this work, he was given the chance to change what he did. He asked if he could work on the other side of the cars doing the same thing. So he installed tires on the right side for a couple of weeks and realized how unhappy he was. With his supervisor's permission, he went back to the left and his familiar state of well-being.

What my mechanic had discovered was that the Swedish culture believes that *things* have souls. For the tire installer, his job was the completion of the creation of a new soul in the form of an automobile. He was the doctor delivering the baby and, I'm guessing, the one who last touched the car before it went out into the world. Hence the strength of his feeling about his job. Which may account for why I have named my own Saabs Sven, Emeralda and Zumuela (zoom-away-la). I also have Mona, a 1970 Land Rover that I've had since 1974. She has seen me through every one of my relationships and was the vehicle that my son used to learn how to drive. If he could handle double-clutching into second gear, he could handle anything. Now she takes me across the dirt roads on the mesas of the Southwest bouncing along and feeling right at home.

When I was around eight years old, I met Gerow Smiley at the Mohonk Mountain House in upstate New York. He strummed his guitar and played the music of Woody Guthrie along with the songs of the accompanying folk movement. I was hooked. Thanks to my father's membership in the Columbia Record Club, I was already familiar with Bob Dylan and Peter, Paul & Mary. But the thought of playing music live was as thrilling as anything I can remember. For me, this was the beginning of self-sufficiency. At eleven, I was given a guitar and started learning songs from listening to records. Every day after school and homework, I played. What I was really doing was entering the world of emotions through art. Bathing in everything from joy to sadness to humor or the blues is when I still feel most at home emotionally.

Right now, there is a sense that I'm going through the motions doing the things I love: swimming, playing music, teaching dance, reading poetry on the radio, talking to friends and writing. Underneath there is a current of grief that began almost three weeks ago. It's like a slow melodic counterpoint to the normal pulse of living. That combination of a slow melody coupled with a fast rhythm in music bypasses all of my filters creating a preciousness that is so dear to me. I couldn't tell you what that grief was about so I am riding the wave hanging on trying to keep my balance. The activities I mentioned keep me grounded so the grief can ride its own wave to wherever it needs to go.

When I swim laps, the silky feel of the water is the most reassuring touch in my life at the moment. A few years ago, I began to close my eyes every time I took a breath. I open them again underwater. This method can bring on a meditative mindset that alters time. Between the water's texture, forgotten time and being in motion, I'm usually in heaven, another world.

There is a recent trend that concerns me greatly. Through someone else's public admission of the traumas of their life, I feel like I'm being bludgeoned into entering the story and, in turn, the world of that particular person. For instance, the recovering addict is often given celebrity status while existing celebrities are now expected to reveal their own dark nights of the soul through memoir writing and interview tours. What was once considered personal and private is now fodder for book sales and notoriety. This feeds into the cultural idea of a need for specialness to differentiate one from another. It's strange to see this fascination with the dark side of humanity as if it was a newly discovered country. The dark aspect has always been there all along but with the diminishment of the importance of an inner life, any admission of internal struggle seems to imply some sort of extraordinary courage. Is there anyone who hasn't been traumatized? There is a tribe mentality that has arisen through this identification with a particular trauma. It's as if we are looking for yet new ways to identify ourselves and identify with each other. The worlds I'm referring to don't care about identity. These worlds care about resonance.

What do you love regardless of whether others are present or not? These are the places we enter secretly and alone which prefer a confidentiality that might be revealed very selectively, if at all. That could be with a very close friend or an intimate partner, through your art, or shared in the exploration and creation of that world. Yet once you go public with the personal, the mystery is lost, the literal world floods back in and whatever sacred energy was created has to be diminished.

A kora (West African stringed harp) player came to town a year ago and performed with a percussionist and a cellist. He is originally from Senegal and a family of kora players. I think of this instrument, along with the mbira (Zimbabwean finger piano), as the preference of the angels. To dance to this music may be the closest I've ever come to ecstasy. Dancing is always a conversation between my body and what I'm hearing and feeling. If I don't feel it, I don't move. This particular night with the kora player, I was wonderfully surprised at the variation and complexity of how my body was responding. And the kora player was feeding off my movement. On and on it went like talking to a new friend late into the night. We were discovering connections by turning the unknown into the known and back to the unknown again. How I love these other worlds.

Nurturing The Soul

Some scientists believe that the full effects of climate change will be upon us by 2030 if there is no concerted effort to alter human behavior. What does that mean? Instead of a handful of events a year such as hurricanes, typhoons, wildfires, drought and flooding, catastrophes will become the everyday norm, not the exception. Like any living organism, the earth is responding accordingly to our behavior on, above, and below its surface. There is a hard reality here in which we are all complicit. Capitalism, by its nature, focuses on the immediate bottom line, a monetary interest rather than an environmentally sustainable future. In turn, lifestyles have been created that most of us have come to enjoy, even expect as a birthright. What we once thought of as business as usual is no longer healthy for the planet we call our home. This is an existential threat that only rivals the proliferation of nuclear weapons. Without a place that is livable, all the other issues go away.

We live in a time when dysfunction has become normalized. This is most prevalent in government responses, or lack thereof, around the world to the needs of its citizens. In the

United States, those existential threats mentioned above barely show up on the political radar. Astonishing! How rare it is for me to hear anyone talking about carbon footprints anymore. What I discovered recently was that the world climate summits have left no footprint thanks to buying carbon offsets. In essence, those offsets pay for the planting of trees, for instance, that will eliminate carbon to the extent that it was created by the user. Imagine booths offering these offsets at all of our airports and gas stations.

Some external solutions have already been offered. Hopefully, many more will come but I want to talk about a way to cope with our situation internally and how that can reflect back into the world. Action in the world is useful if it comes from the right place. For a moment, consider the state of the planet as a reflection of your own soul. Are there extinctions taking place? How alive and in tune is your curiosity, your movement, your cooperation, your openness? Why can't most of us *feel* the loss of life after a tsunami on the other side of the world? What has happened to our instincts that no longer allow us to read the natural world accurately without some electronic device? Can we discern between information, entertainment and pollution in our lives? Where has balance been lost? There is an old idea that the extent to which we relinquish our own wildness parallels the extent to which we abandon or tame the natural wilderness. How fully alive do you want to be?

Imagination without a profit motive is the very ground that has been lost. This ground is the terrain of the soul which is flexible and can create compromise if needed. Imagine whimsically writing a love letter to yourself by sitting in the sun, eyes closed and feeling the breeze instead of checking a text message or breaking news. Yes, institutions are crumbling, the shadows of our violence towards others and the earth have returned to haunt us. Hope has been put on the endangered species list, but the creation of anything new comes from chaos. This is why the soul's imagining might be our best and most accessible way onward.

That can only happen once we learn to nurture our souls. Unfortunately, our culture does not actively embrace this idea. Cultural anthropologist Angeles Arrien shared four questions created by Indigenous cultures for soul retrieval. When was the last time you sang? When was the last time you danced? When was the last time you sat in silence? And when was the last time you were enchanted by a story—particularly your own? Your answers will determine to what extent you are in touch with this deeper aspect of yourself. Then the work begins in determining where one has created false beliefs—which become defenses for survival—and where one has been wounded psychologically or indoctrinated culturally. For a moment, envision that the world *is* coming to an end. What is it you are willing to do to become the full potential of your innermost being?

Dealing with your issues is essential. Creating balance with those things that bring you joy is equally important. Self-care is a full-time occupation so that the inner life of the soul can determine the outer life of our identity rather than the other way around. This is where practice, discipline and discernment are useful so that you don't get lost in consensual reality. For instance, screen time has become an addiction in western culture. Whenever we are looking at a screen, we are no longer connecting to the natural world which perhaps allows us the best template; the place where *anyone* can learn adaptation, patience, humility, surrender, sanctuary, a sense of knowing what's enough and an understanding of the cooperation of species within what appears to be chaos. How would you compare the amount of your technological time to your moments in nature?

Nurturing the soul helps us to discover what our individual gifts might be and how they could be shared with the world. Knowing this creates a cherishing of those gifts along with the self-care needed to maintain and grow this precious part of yourself. If we could grieve the dozens of species who were lost today alone, our subsequent actions might alter from business as usual. The answers are no longer coming from our trusted institutions. Technology, for all its power and glory, has caused its own share of harm. Since that is the case, it's up to each one of us to do the work of nurturing. Bringing ourselves into balance, first individually, then with the world, is how nature works. In turn, nurturing our souls connects us to the natural world and therefore nurtures the planet. Awareness of the strength and fragility of our souls is the very understanding that helps us to cross over to caring for others and the earth. Teaching this would demonstrate to our children that they deserve a future as well.

A Way Forward

The horrific tragedy in Parkland, Florida has unleashed a tsunami of blame; lack of gun control, failure of the FBI to heed warnings regarding the shooter, scarcity of mental health care, and Hollywood's depiction of violence. It's like reaching for frayed threads without ever touching the body of the fabric. Maybe the time has come to face the fact that, as a culture, we have been unconsciously complicit in the creation of these events.

Let's start with the belief that violence is generally acceptable as a way to resolve conflict, to promote an agenda or to express unresolved personal issues. Schools don't teach this, our society does. We have the largest military in the world that has less to do with peace than with defending, often through force, a lifestyle. We also have an equally large entertainment industry—supported by our ticket sales, television subscriptions and Internet connections—that thrives, in part, on the thrill of bloodshed. In tandem, there is the language of assault created through a shame-and-blame mentality. This psychological abuse is most prevalent with our politicians. Someone is right and someone is wrong. Add our Puritan background to the mix and the result is that the wrongdoer, whoever that may be, deserves to be punished.

Between 1982 and 2021, 97 percent of the shooters have been male. Studies show that the masculine brain is not fully developed until the age of twenty-five; impulse control being the final step to full maturation. So many of the perpetrators have not had a full ability to reason or feel. Indigenous people used rites of initiation as a way to transition youth into mature adults. In the case of my discussion, the young Indigenous male was prepared to some extent for this passage. But that did not guarantee his survival, for instance, during a three-month solo "walkabout" in the Australian outback. Maturing into an adult implies not only physical growth, but emotional, psychological, spiritual, ethical and moral maturation as well. Does a civilian possessing a budding nineteen-year-old brain ever need to hold a killing machine like an AR-15 in their hands? Is there any example in the natural world where the intentional killing of innocents takes place? Is an armed society a civil society?

The poet, Robert Bly, offers the idea that once men left the fields in favor of the factories during the Industrial Revolution, their conversations between each other were, for the most part, irretrievably altered or simply vanished. This is significant. As a result, many men I know today are struggling with the thought of how to be a man, as well as with how to have deep conversations with women. In my generation, the 1950s male continued to be the model, prioritizing sternness and mechanical adeptness over vulnerability and being in touch with feelings, imagination and intuition.

Just when that model was settling in, the Feminist Movement came along in the late 1960s in an attempt to level the playing field in terms of equal pay, job opportunity, owning property, maternity leave and holding office, for instance. There was no significant parallel men's movement to offer an alternative to the strong, stern model. Women were demanding their rights to equality while many men were not willing to relinquish the power and traditions that had created the imbalance. So the opportunity for a collective male initiation through the zeitgeist was lost. I'm still grieving that loss.

To paraphrase Carl Jung, whatever we don't deal with inside will show up outside as our fate. I wouldn't say that most people condone the use of violence or the ownership of military style weapons. But we tolerate it. On the other hand, shame and blame is as commonplace as smartphone use. At what point in time will we make it personal by refraining from judgment as a first option, by not patronizing a film that has a picture of a weapon on the publicity poster, by not cutting off another driver when commuting and by taking our children outdoors to learn from nature instead of allowing more screen time with a violent video game? The return to civility is going to take some work and individual responsibility.

Since we learn most of these behaviors from our parents, our friends and our culture, maybe rethinking what we teach primarily at home and, to a lesser extent, in our schools is a way forward. What are we doing to create adults who are in touch with their humanity? In the case of the school shootings, violence is usually a symptom of unresolved anger and isolation. Why not make anger management a mandatory class during middle school? We could be helping our children with ways to investigate their beliefs as well. How about explaining non-violent (some call it compassionate) communication, healthy relationships, a return to art programs that promote imagination to compliment linear thinking, good nutrition, the care of one's body beyond athletics and, the big one, peace. Beyond parenting, I'm certain that there are veterans and elders who would be more than willing to help with that topic.

It's unrealistic to think we can go back to initiation as practiced in the past. Most humans are no longer in touch with nature enough to have a willingness (or the survival skills) to learn what she has to offer. This is a real loss. Nature works through cooperation and adaptation. As in the case of the Parkland tragedy, the development of killing technology has far surpassed the emotional and psychological development of a nineteen-year-old male. If no one is willing to put a lid on that technology, then how do we catch up developmentally with our inner lives? The anthropologist Gregory Bateson said, "The major problems in the world are the result of the difference between how nature works and the way people think." It's time to completely revisit our relationship to violence.

Without Initiation

It is not a good time to be a white male. The modern track record is dismal in terms of harm towards others. There's Harvey Weinstein, Roger Ailes, Bill O'Reilly, Bernie Madoff, John Stumpf, Larry Nassar, Nicolas Cruz, Dylan Roof, James Holmes, Adam Lanza, Cardinal Law, Derek Chauvin and the 97 percent of school shooters who have been white men or, in some cases, boys. And that is exactly the problem; our culture has no intentional method or process of maturing boys into men. This applies to girls and women as well but the results have been nowhere near as damaging. Not that all women have or will become mothers, but the experience of pregnancy and childbirth may serve as an initiation in itself with the inherent risks of death for mother and child along with the need for subsequent nurturing of both to sustain life. There is no parallel undertaking for men. Humility learned through pain is a powerful teacher, along with the wisdom gained through the experience.

I've spent most of my life just trying to figure out *how* to be a man; first as a way to be comfortable with myself, then with other men and finally with post-feminist women. My father, as my first role model, had adopted the stern parenting approach which he learned from his father. This came down through German ancestry which was very much a part of the old European idea that a man is the king of his castle. As my father used to say, "No ifs, ands or buts." In other words, decisions could never be discussed, challenged or, God forbid, created through consensus. So this dictatorial aspect instilled an automatic reflex within me that authority couldn't be trusted and should always be questioned. In retrospect, it was a wonderful lesson, inadvertently, on the value of inquiry.

To give a more rounded picture, all of the things my father *didn't* try to consciously teach turned into his richest legacy. In almost sixty years of marriage, I'm certain that he was always faithful to my mother. Part of that had to do with his generation but in relation to modern marriage, it was exceptional. Endurance at work was similar. Rarely did I see him take a sick day. And we were partners in washing and cleaning the two cars—a sedan for his work and a station wagon for the family—every Sunday which may have been his closest thing to religion. Above all, he took us to the Catskill and Shawangunk Mountains which surrounded our hometown and, in the summers, we experienced the Atlantic Ocean on the shores of Cape Cod. I learned to love these land and seascapes which have stayed with me ever since.

After I challenged his authority, my father threatened to send me to military school to "straighten me out" as a way of initiation into his version of reality. Actually, I was the son who did my chores, did my homework and made my bed. As my mother tells it, I was her one child (out of four) she never had to worry about because all I did in my early years was sing and dance. I was blessed with a happy soul. That didn't make it easier when I had to encounter the social world of going to school. There was yet more authority and the whole new challenge of interacting with girls, and later women. In high school, I remember being asked what I wanted to do with my life and having absolutely no idea. This was during the late 1960s and my questioning had become allies with the Civil Rights Movement, as well as the feminist, anti-war, new music and spirituality movements.

My first real male decisions happened when I had earned enough to buy a Martin twelve-string and later a Martin six-string guitar in 1969 and 1971, respectively. Around that same time, the first two albums I ever bought were Joni Mitchell's *Song To A Seagull* and the debut Moby Grape release. The diversity and musicality of both those recordings has defined my musical taste ever since. I guess I could have worked towards becoming a professional musician with the skills and sensibility that I had created but I didn't care for the lifestyle and many of the other, mostly male, musicians I knew. In high school I participated in the team sports of tennis, skiing and soccer rather than baseball, basketball and football. Between my curiosity and becoming an outsider, I wasn't a typical male.

My example, regardless of the outcome, illustrates a complete lack of deliberate initiation for boys like me in America. We have been and still are trained to be productive, emotionally disconnected, linear thinkers who often have no relationship to poetic or aesthetic sensibilities much less moral or ethical concerns—in other words, to become good citizens of a capitalist society. If you are making money, your place is assured, even if it may not be entirely legal. The stern father model mentioned earlier compliments the 1950s male that used a post-World War II military mentality as a basis for masculinity. It's still very much alive today in the conservative movement and in the size of the budget of the Department of Defense.

Our fractured idea of maleness is revealing itself more and more in the behaviors of sexual predators who are finally being held to account, police officers who are indiscriminately killing men and women of color, those committing financial malfeasance, corrupt politicians, perpetrators of domestic violence, and, angry young men who resort to blowing up buildings and killing innocent children in schools. Is it any wonder that drug and alcohol abuse are so prevalent in America? For our boys in particular, we are not teaching them about the presence and nurturing of their souls. This is what initiation did for Aboriginal societies. But the boys and men who have caused so much harm to others within our society certainly have souls that are lost.

The older Indigenous initiations created a testing of a young man through ritual and the ambivalence of the natural and spirit worlds. If young men didn't have their skills together, they perished. Just like in nature, it was survival of the fittest. Sadly, we no longer have the conscious contact or reverence for nature and those unseen energies that often direct the course of our lives. All the men who have caused harm were under the illusion that they were in control and can impose that control on anyone or anything around them. This is the potential curse that is part of the baggage of being an uninitiated white male.

The point of initiation, in whatever form, is a maturing ritual that creates a deep, integrated awareness of a personal responsibility first towards oneself and the earth then towards the community and the extending culture. Within that responsibility is the understanding that any harm to the earth or its inhabitants, beyond survival, is forbidden if one is to stay within that community. For example, past Hawaiian cultures would condemn anyone to death if one of these sacred laws was violated. With the acts of those men mentioned at the beginning of this essay, we are now witnessing the loss of that sacredness in modern culture. Since the larger community can no longer imagine or uphold this reverence, the focus becomes more and more on the individual male to discover then find their own way to the moral, ethical, emotional, psychological and spiritual maturity of the adult to become a living example for all of those who follow.

Differences

The history of men and women in America can seem like two parallel streams that intersect only for the sake of procreation, raising a family and preserving a culture. For Caucasians, the European model of male dominance has been the cultural standard which is only just beginning to unravel due to the feminist and, more recently, the #MeToo movements. None of this could have taken place without the demands of the suffragettes at the beginning of the twentieth century and the passage of the nineteenth Amendment to the United States Constitution in 1920. At stake were not just voting rights but the eventual hope of a level playing field. Much work has taken place since with much more still needed.

The lack of initiation in modern culture has had a profound effect on the maturation of men. Maturity is now gauged in terms of diplomas, degrees and awards. In others words, success relative to age, rather than wisdom. In Indigenous tribes, men were involved with routine, ritual and specific acts of physical violence that included body decoration, hunting and war. These can still exist somewhat today as acts of prowess but without any spiritual or mythological connection. Testosterone has not been used to mature but to dominate since the rise of patriarchal societies. Conversely, First Nation tribes that had initiation rituals for males revered their grandmothers as the final word in any important matter giving reverence and power to older females.

In Robert Bly's book, *Iron John,* he presents the idea that the conversation between men came to a halt during the Industrial Revolution once work in the fields was replaced by work in factories. Men working in nature alongside each other is much more conducive to talking than having one repetitious task at a noisy machine. In contrast, women never had such a fissure. Instead, their conversations have kept on going. Bly, along with James Hillman and Michael Meade, made a bold attempt to create a male movement in response to feminism; they did this with their writings and workshops that suggested a path forward through mythology, psychology and poetic sensibility. The implication was that by redirecting the male focus, humility and new purpose could diminish the unquestioned regimes of arrogance, dominance and privilege. It was a big leap that had a profound effect on me, perhaps due to the coincidental timing of the events in my own life. I can tell you firsthand as an older white male that those men who have done their own work which might parallel the strides of the women's movement are few and far between.

I grew up with a stern father who mirrored the behavior of his own stern father. Discussion, mutual cooperation or, God forbid, questioning of authority were all never a consideration. At sixteen, I began to question that authority out loud. This was the beginning of my outward contempt for power due to title but without justification. It was also the conscious beginning of coming to terms with the bottomless grief caused by the distances between my father and myself. This grief may be the perfect snapshot of where so many men are today. We still long for approval and love from our fathers who were never taught, or even considered, that a male could be both masculine *and* nurturing. Wasn't nurturing the woman's job?

Critics of the men's movement say that it was all about getting in touch with our feelings and being more sensitive. Admirable goals for anyone which is why they are humanist, not gender-related qualities. Yes, men *do* tend to be stuck in their heads. It was the only thing I could do growing up in order to survive in an emotional desert. My salvation came through imagination found in the arts. Yet the question isn't about feelings and sensitivity. It's perhaps more importantly about our very identities and what beliefs are at the foundation. Which brings up the central quandary; without any questioning of the beliefs regarding dominance and privilege, how can men possibly expect to keep pace with women who are rightfully demanding a full expression of their own potential? I'm talking about reinventing oneself in relation to the zeitgeist. If women have already been doing this for the past century, isn't it high time for men to do their work as well?

To give some perspective here, there are plenty of females who want the benefits of feminism without the risk. There are also those women who don't mind the 1950s male model which is so predictable thereby making these men easy to maneuver around or manipulate. I've seen this behavior where women are silently running the show without shattering the rigid male archetype that prevails. Things get done but nothing moves. The business-as-usual approach has birthed the questioning of any number of institutions—the church, government, marriage, education, employment and gender identity—that have relied on this old dynamic. Even the consistency of climate can no longer be taken for granted. We now live in that brave new world where one has to adapt or perish.

There seem to be two very different conversations going on right now. Men are still looking for a way to begin a conversation beyond politics, sports and repairing or dominating something while women are actively engaging in conversations about the most essential things including family, safety, emotions and equal rights as humans. While men are just looking for words, women are adding new chapters to the book of the future. Until my fellow males do the hard work of unraveling power-based beliefs that have caused harm to humans and the planet, not much will change until the possibility of our eventual extinction as humans is a big enough threat. Perhaps that thought will be an incentive to do the work. Then a new conversation might take place between men and women that includes honesty, sincerity, equanimity and compassion—a conversation that could lead to more equitable societies.

The Deepening Divide

I've never lived in a city with a population greater than thirty thousand, the population of my hometown of Kingston, New York. The Big Apple was just ninety miles south, which is where I would go to concerts, see films and buy guitars. A visit was always enough. I didn't care for all of the noise or the crowds. I'm not averse to urban areas but my need to be near nature and wilderness has been an important part of keeping in touch with myself.

The United States Office of Management and Budget makes a distinction between micropolitan (population between ten thousand and fifty thousand) and metropolitan (population over fifty thousand) statistical areas. As of 2016, the estimate is that 86 percent of the United States population was found in metropolitan areas which includes the surrounding sprawl. That is over double what it was fifty years ago. There's a lot to extrapolate here (economic migration, the vibrancy of cities, attraction to the power centers of culture), but one thing for certain is that Americans are more urban and less involved directly with nature, than ever. It's as if two very different tribes have developed that sometimes mingle with each other.

I now live near Taos, New Mexico where the population of the whole county is slightly larger than my hometown. There is an eclectic mix of Native Americans (5 percent), Hispanics and Mexican (52 percent), Anglos (40 percent) and mixed races (3 percent). This is not your typical American community. When I see visitors to Taos in a grocery store, it's apparent that they are not from here. Part of it is the clothing, the hair styles and maybe the car in waiting that's blocking other cars when there is plenty of parking available. This is not a judgment since I feel and probably look just as out of place when visiting a city.

Does any of this make a difference? Not much if you remain in your own environment. My concern is that as the population moves further away from nature while becoming more reliant on technology, our own behaviors seem to be changing accordingly. Silence and solitude are great casualties of our time in the population centers which may account for the rise of meditation practices and retreats as compensation. How does the intuitive and instinctual life, beyond fear, evolve if one isn't ever without distraction? The same applies to being present and in the moment. Imagination seems to have benefited somewhat from new creation tools and venues now available, along with immediate access to a vast amount of information. But the emotional body may be losing the most ground simply because there is too much content available. From natural disasters, school shootings, Middle East war, immigrant tragedy, loss of faith in our institutions; the list goes on but to have the time or energy to process all of this information found through a multitude of sources is simply impossible. Add to that the busy pace of urban life and the stress becomes insurmountable without nature as a potential release and antidote.

Years ago after graduating from college, I spent a summer teaching tennis in Vermont. When I was young, the sport was accessible to anyone due to free municipal courts being available in most towns. My favorite clients were older people who just wanted to hit the ball back and forth without ever playing a game or keeping score. Those volleys could last up to thirty minutes long. It was like dancing. In contrast, there was one man, among many, who had come up from Boston and just wanted to kill the ball by hitting it as hard as he could over and over. After about ten minutes of that, I remember walking up to the net and suggesting that we get a six-pack of beer so that he could relax and have some fun. Redirecting stress isn't the same as release.

Stress is the new normal and rising in America. How does it show up? When I'm on the streets and in the stores of a city or at an airport, I've noticed three things: few if any are smiling, there is little or no eye contact and spatial awareness near other people is no longer a priority. This applies to driving a car as well. Everything from lack of attention to outright aggression has become commonplace. The average commuter now spends about forty-two hours a year in traffic jams. A friend in Massachusetts told me a common rationale for not using a turn signal when changing lanes on a crowded highway: "Never reveal your intentions to the enemy." If you were cutting off someone you knew, you might think twice before acting.

Is this separateness in lifestyles any different than in the past? Beyond the loss of civility, I don't think so. But there is an escalation in the differences due to the very distinct paces and focus of urban and non-urban lifestyles. Basically, people from urban areas—from federal government, business, education, entertainment and media industries—are in control. An overriding mindset has been created insisting on "busy is better" and that politics and economics will always dominate the news cycle unless a catastrophe has taken place. Implied within this mindset are the false beliefs that happiness can be found in specific ways: through being busy (i.e. productive), whether the economy is growing or not and if my political party is in office. Of course mainstream news is focused on people mostly found in cities. Does our compassion need to be limited?

Living closer to nature *can* make a difference. Having the sunrise and sunset to witness every day is healing. To see walking rain across the desert in the summer leaves me in a state of wonder. Hearing a coyote howling outside at night is simply thrilling. This is not to say that Taos and other rural areas don't have their own share of problems including drug use, gangs, domestic violence, teenage pregnancy and poverty. But the rural pace allows for openness, creativity and slowing down enough to perhaps create an ease of mind.

Curiously, the United States has fallen from third to seventeenth place in the past ten years according to the World Happiness Report. Social concerns far outweigh personal economics. The report cites "rising inequality, corruption, isolation, and distrust" as the causes for the deterioration of personal well-being. "The major problems in the world are the result of the difference between how nature works and the way people think." (Gregory Bateson, Anthropologist) Maybe we are doing something terribly wrong. The climate seems to be saying so, as does the Great Pacific Garbage

Patch which is now estimated to be twice the size of the state of Texas. Last year, a friend said that he never imagined that the dying of the Great Barrier Reef in Australia would take place within his lifetime. I'm sure that the residents of Puerto Rico, the United States Virgin Islands, Houston and the West Coast of the United States would have something to say about the aftereffects of unprecedented events in nature.

Yesterday, I spent about four hours hiking in the Rio Grande del Norte National Monument. I saw twelve people in that time. Everyone said hello. It's an odd thing to admit that I feel safer and more comfortable in nature than I do around other people. During the most difficult times in my life, I have found the most solace in the woods or by the water. When I reached the confluence of the Rio Grande and the Rio Pueblo, I sat and had lunch watching and listening to the pulse of the river. There was a green tint to the water which was otherwise clear while at the same time reflecting the blue of the sky when viewed from the right angle. I recalled the luck I had once to see river otters diving in and out of the water as they worked their way upstream. It looked like effortless play. I would have traded places in a minute. What was the attraction? Unlike anything I could ever experience in a city, these sleek, spirited animals possessed one of the things everyone seems to be looking for—the unconfined space to be free.

A Letter to the World

(December 2016)

Dear World, I'm feeling uncertain about whatever transitions are taking place in America. But I want to give you an update from my vantage point in rural New Mexico.

Democracy has been and was meant to be an evolving form of governance, a living organism. We are still trying to discover (or invent) who we are. The positive side of this is a possibility of creating a situation where old and new ideas can ignite innovation and the hope of a genuine freedom. The problem is that we have perhaps grown a little too enamored of ourselves. Despite laws and treaties, we are barely coming to grips with our own history of abuse and disenfranchisement of anyone of color, as well as of women. Perhaps we need an annual symbolic "Day of Amends" where white males, myself included, say "I'm sorry" silently or out loud to anyone of color and to women, even if it's just a gesture.

We live in an era where time itself feels compressed. You may have noticed how the values of technology are weakening a moral sense and overtaking the values we need to be fully human. Speed and efficiency clearly outpace the patience required for caring and understanding. As much as we all participate in the modern world, I long for those wait-a-minute moments when our plates were less full with meals easier to digest.

Add to that the enormity of changes taking place as a result of this accelerated time frame. Marriage and gender identity were rarely questioned thirty years ago. Those days are over, along with the possibility of working hard so one can afford to buy their own home. That dream has yet to be reconfigured. We are the land of technological innovation but we haven't kept current with similar strides in terms of emotional intelligence and psychological adaptation. Our bodies and souls have been left behind. The progressives always want progress, while the conservatives feel more comfortable with what they know and have known. I'm no longer sure myself if all progress is in our best interests. I still own music on vinyl, along with a 1970 Land Rover that is driven regularly.

I recall a story about someone asking Carl Jung if there was any hope for Western civilization. Dr. Jung replied, "Yes, but only if enough people do their inner work." One area where America has surpassed the rest of the world is through the sheer volume of information and entertainment now available. But has that volume become too noisy and just a distraction? The focus is almost always outward. Even with our relative abundance, we would prefer to dwell on reading and math scores as priorities in education, for instance, rather than encouraging children to remain curious. And our news is dominated by politics, economics, violence and natural catastrophe. I'd like to suggest a news story on the casualties of curiosity, wonder and imagination in our culture.

Yes, I'm grieving here. America has always been at its best when we're helping others regardless of borders. Imagine if participating in the Peace Corps or some other volunteer enterprise would be required of everyone as part of being a citizen of the United States? We seem to be at our worst when we lose sight of that kind of caring. Oh world, I think that capitalism has gotten the best of us. But I could also give you numerous examples of everyday kindness and compassion which you rarely see in the news.

I wonder what it would look like if we, as individual citizens of America, applied new ways and language to our modern psyches and lives? How fluid might we be if we had the courage and curiosity to challenge our beliefs periodically, to know when to set boundaries and when to surrender and to know when new values and beliefs might be needed depending on the circumstance?

Underneath our system, capitalism relies on production and consumption. Democracy, based on the power of the individual, implies the possibility of freedom and the "pursuit of happiness." But the latter isn't working out for everyone. What if love found through compassion, kindness, patience, humility, gratitude, praise, forgiveness and service governed our lives through the lens of a fresh democracy? We made it to the moon. Maybe we can all reach this far star.

I know it looks like we are withdrawing from the world somewhat. Perhaps we've spread ourselves too thin. Maybe the concept of an already interconnected yet polarized country is too much for someone who doesn't know where their next meal is coming from or how to pay their rent? And maybe America just needs some time to consider and hopefully grow out of that polarization if we are all going to continue moving together?

I don't want to apologize to you, world, for where we are as a nation right now. It's just where we are. I'm not sure how any of us keep current with what's going on internally while being in an ever-changing environment. But please bear with us. It's a very exciting time to be alive even with the challenges at hand.

Take care and be well.

Signs

Several years ago, I visited my then ninety-two-year-old mother at her retirement village. The facility is lovely with apartments, a formal dining room and an indoor pool that has the warmth of a hot tub. The residents are in various stages of physical and psychological deterioration since most are in their eighties and a few, like my mother, in their nineties. I spoke to one who had had Alzheimer's disease for a few years. This woman used to play violin in a symphony orchestra as a career. A few days before our conversation, she had fallen, which created a pretty good black eye on the right side. We talked about her eye and what she could remember about her fall which wasn't much. What was remarkable was not the conversation itself but how much laughter erupted while talking. Some of this had to do with the nature of the woman, regardless of her condition. It occurred to me later that for this particular person, Alzheimer's gave the gift of mostly no past, no stories, no future and, ultimately, no worries. As a living embodiment of no attachment, she could go on tour and teach by example.

That example of non-attachment helped when I came

home to find a two-foot-long juvenile rattlesnake curled against the stove island of my kitchen. This was several days after a hike where a two-foot-long garter snake raced across my path during a stream crossing. I didn't know that snakes could swim and stay afloat. In the kitchen, I was surprised and curious but didn't panic. How did a snake get in my house? And did it really want to take up residence on a cold concrete floor? I went to the garage to get a cardboard box to move the reptile but when I returned, it was gone! I looked everywhere and found nothing. So I turned up the music knowing wherever there was noise, I was safe. I found it the next day behind a trash basket in a guest bathroom. I retrieved the box once again then placed it so that the snake was between a wall and the open box. In it went as if on command. I closed it up, went outside then let it loose. About a week later, I found a baby rattlesnake on top of a pile of compost in a bin near where I released the one mentioned above. It instinctually rose up and hissed but, with it only having a length of six inches, I wasn't worried. Familiarity was breeding a strange kind of companionship.

    I grew up in the Hudson Valley of New York where moisture and humidity fall into the East Coast norm. Snakes are scarce. My mother is still there and on my most recent visit that region was as lush from moisture as I've ever seen it. The winter was especially wet followed by a rainy spring. Even without much sun, potted pansies and geraniums on her patio were blooming like the tropics. Here in New Mexico, wildfire season is well under way as of Memorial Day weekend along with the closing of the Santa Fe National Forest on June first. Last night, a new blaze broke out in Ute Park near Cimarron and has already consumed two thousand acres in twenty-four hours. The state is currently in its most severe drought since 1895 when climate records were first recorded. Over on the Big Island of Hawaii, Kilauea has been newly erupting for about a month as of this writing. The lava has covered four-square miles with a couple of streams making it to the ocean. One of those just covered the Kopoho Tide Pools which was a very special place for me. This volcano has been active since 1983. Presaging the hurricane season in the United States, a tropical depression arrived in May on the Gulf Coast which is abnormally early. So many extremes.

Like the lava percolating beneath the earth's crust, there have been several eruptions in terms of human interaction. A recent vote in Ireland legalized abortion. The Catholic Church is being held more and more accountable for the conduct of its priests which parallels the #MeToo movement in going after predatory men. The surviving students of the Parkland, Florida shooting have done more to move the debate over gun control into the public conversation. And something I wondered if I'd ever see in my lifetime was the possibility of gay marriage no longer being a hot topic for debate in America. As beliefs and attitudes change individually, a tipping point is sometimes reached publicly. It's as if government is the last place of change in modern culture which may point to a general loss of faith in what used to be our trusted institutions. As a respite from all of this turmoil, the marriage of Prince Harry to Megan Markle offered an almost fairytale escape. It was fascinating that someone who will never ascend royally in England has begun a life with a mixed-race American actress. How prescient that they kept the political and economic worlds away from the event so that the focus could be, at that moment, on love.

It's spring here in the Rockies and everything from flowers to returning birds are all about one month ahead of schedule. The streams are low, the skies mostly cloudless. The outdoor pool where I swim has been open for a few weeks and though I couldn't tell you why, my skin says that the water has been sumptuous. As I did laps today, I was reminded of swim-filled days during summer vacation as a child when six hours in the water was normal and we would take breaks by lying with our wet bodies on the warm concrete that was surrounding the pool. This may be one of the most comforting things I still do with my body. Our concrete beach next to the chlorinated lake was all ours, even if for a few hours a day. How could I have known that I was already plotting my future from the single digits of my past? Like those snakes I mentioned earlier, so many skins will be shed just to savor the warmth of the sun on my body.

Deeper Currents

Water—my primordial love. As long as it's warm enough, I'm in. Due to the efforts of my father and one of his friends, a small club was created back when I was a child by getting fifty families to contribute one thousand dollars each to buy land then construct a pool and a tennis court. It was there that I first played in the water and was given the luxury of swimming lessons. When talking to my ninety-three-year-old mother the other night, I asked her if she remembered the name of the woman who taught me. Both of us were surprised when she blurted out the name, Pat Tiano. To this day, I'm still grateful for what I learned.

It was at that pool where a summer day camp took place and we would play tag for hours on end. Two things had to be learned: sprinting in the water and climbing out of the pool *fast* by kicking our feet enough while pushing down with our hands on the concrete edge, bringing a knee or foot up to finish the job. Looking back, what shape we must have been in. The secret reward for this motion was lying down on the sun-warmed concrete with our drenched bodies. It's a version of heaven that only some lap swimmers and most children know of and understand.

At Lake Mohonk, New York, I became a lifeguard in the summer which included the responsibility of leading a swim across the lake, about one-third of a mile. Since various levels of hopefully competent swimmers would participate, I would do everything from a crawl to the breaststroke to treading water to lead and keep the pack together. Sprinting at the childhood pool transformed into endurance which may be a metaphor for getting older. I was inadvertently learning about distance and pacing myself. Who knew that I would become a lap swimmer in years to come?

After college, there was a period without swimming probably due to poverty and all that was required to survive winters in Vermont. In my youthful ambition, my first autumn there was spent bucking and hand splitting seven cords of wood to heat a log cabin that perched on the ridge of Roxbury Gap. There was an outhouse which was preferred over the indoor chemical toilet that just created more work to maintain and empty. My outdoor record, as well as, limit, was sixteen degrees below zero. Two winters later, after thirty days of no sun in January and no temperature above zero, it was time to move west.

Colorado had been calling since I was already in a ski bum mode back east. How affectionately I look back at those days when one could pursue a passion on a shoe-string budget. We were still skiing in blue jeans! The memory is like reading an old love letter with its innocence, energy and verve. The Vail Valley became my new home and where I got married and had a son. Forty-five minutes to the west was Glenwood Springs with the worlds largest outdoor hot spring-fed pool. At one end were four lap lanes wide enough to accommodate multiple swimmers. With a water temperature of ninety degrees, I could swim year-round regardless of weather. Here was the beginning of my distance swimming. Though it didn't happen often, I found myself gliding along in the warm water during the middle of a snowstorm.

I have a friend who grew up in Denver and now says that the best thing about Colorado is New Mexico. The Vail Valley was simply getting too crowded, too focused on tourism, too far away from the arts on a grass roots level. I moved to Taos in 2002 and immediately found pools to continue my laps. In the fall, winter and spring, I went to Ojo Caliente once a week to swim in their outdoor pool early in the day to avoid casual traffic. That water could be eighty-nine degrees if everything was working properly. No, there weren't any lap lanes but, as I said to myself, "Welcome to New Mexico."

The point to this historical travelogue is a personal discovery. As a kid, I swam for fun with the occasional competition. As a lifeguard, I swam as a job. In Colorado, I was swimming to keep in shape but also to unwind from my job as a property manager. Once I retired and moved south, movement was still important but I began to work on my strokes and incorporating a glide in between. Was effortless effort possible? With that elusive goal, something deeper emerged just after my father died. Immersed in grief, I remember getting in the water, early July, and beginning the crawl. For me, that kind of sorrow alters time, stretches it out and slows it down. It was like swimming in the comfort of my own tears, wishing I could go on forever without having to get out and face the hard reality of no longer having a parent I could talk to or see again. What was this deeper rhythm that I was getting in touch with?

My father's death opened a door through grief that showed me the pulse of my own soul. I had no idea that it was there all along, no idea at the time that I would be writing a book about an inner life. Now when I swim, it's never about muscle or strength per se. Occasionally, strangers come up to ask how long I go. I tell them, "two hours," but that's not the destination. What I'm looking for is that elusive thing called grace. Getting in the pool, beginning a stroke, I know I'm often still in the pace of being in a car, a locker room, perhaps a social interaction or two. The water always reflects an inner rhythm while washing the world away, leaving me with my solitude and the possibility of finding the deeper current that sometimes allows a dream to arise, a moment of calm delight or the vision of light filtering through the ripples of the water created while moving forward.

I-See-Um

The recent no-see-um season has felt like a barbarian invasion with attendant battle scars openly revealed in the aisles of the grocery stores. My own dentist showed me half-inch welt rings above his sock line giving new meaning to the idea of natural selection. Maybe, in the open spiritual tradition of Taos, these flying tormentors have come to teach us all about nondiscrimination. Or that immigration is not an exclusively human issue. Facts can be so pesky when it comes to denial.

Thanks to being partly sequestered in my house during this onslaught, I did a little bit of research to discover some interesting facts. Our mini-raptors are part of the fly family specifically known as Ceratopogonidae or biting midges. There are up to five thousand subspecies with sightings as remote as Mt. Everest. Males and females use plant nectar for food while the females rely on blood meal in order to make babies—up to four hundred at a time, five to seven hatchings in a lifetime. They love light and are especially attracted to the odors of carbon dioxide and lactic acid. So if you are a breathing, moving human who happens to be outdoors, you're on the menu.

Once again, the complexity of women wins the day since the men are only vegan while their mates are both vegan *and* vampires. (The old school guys sitting around the bar will have a heyday with that one.) In defense of the mothers, their agendas have never been hidden. Also, no-see-ums (along with gull midges) are what pollinate the cacao tree which produces cocoa beans to make, yes, chocolate. Maybe a few welts and some itching are the karmic debt for our indulgences?

I've realized two things: regular window screens are as fun as jumping turnstiles in New York City for these minute beings and that they love anything that emits light. So a few nights ago, as a defensive move, I kept the windows closed and lights off and plugged in a guitar to play by the soft glow coming from a sound processor and an amplifier. Just like glamping!

Once I risk leaving the safety of my home, I have a few options. There is gooping up with repellant along with long sleeves, pants, socks, hat and a taser in order to work outside. Or swimming laps which is a perfect refuge: wet body, no bugs. Or going hiking in the high country where spring azure butterflies are much more pleasing flying companions. Or simply buying groceries where I can compare wounds with my friends and neighbors. Thank you to all of the local stores for your air conditioning.

Which brings up the obvious question: What makes Taos so attractive for a couple of weeks a year? It certainly isn't the bike trails, the few remaining live music venues or the dwindling theater scene. I'm just guessing, but perhaps it's the fabulous northern New Mexican landscape, the outdoor restaurant patios and lots of humans. That and the perfect combination of a wet spring and warm temperatures.

Since this is something that can be expected yearly, why not put the wheels of marketing into motion? Here are some ideas: Taos—Apocalypse Now; Taos—Huge Views, Small Problems; Taos—Where The Unseen Is Apparent; Taos—How Good Is Your Repellant? Now we could have the Lillac Festival then Memorial Day weekend followed by the June Swatfest. How about the Solstice No-See-Um Stampede? Might as well have some fun with it.

Maybe I'm getting tired of living in a defensive mode. There's that nondiscrimination lesson. And maybe it's time to move on, honor that Joy Harjo, a Native American from the Muscogee Nation, has been named poet laureate of the United States which may be a good reason to celebrate summer, the blossoming of the year and that anything is still possible.

Aesthetic Considerations

> *Aesthetic enrichment is not a major consideration in the United States.*
>
> — Frank Zappa

Did a perspective of enrichment ever exist in America? I believe that it did during the creation of a new form of government that hoped to emulate the possibilities already possessed within the land, the forests, the mountains, the lakes and the rivers. The physical separation from Europe and its traditions by the Atlantic Ocean helped with this process. There is a beauty to the democratic ideal that mirrors nature where diversity and adaptation exist cooperatively. With our current disconnection from the natural world in favor of urban areas and technology, there is a parallel shift away from elegance towards functionality and data. One can see this through the loss of art programs in early education. Linear thinking is given much more weight than creativity and the world of imagination. The imaginal life is often relegated to the entertainment industry. Even then, Hollywood, television, mainstream music and book publishing have all become increasingly formulaic.

I grew up in the 1950s which was a golden era of style and design. I'm referring to the Fender Stratocaster and Gibson Les Paul guitars which helped usher in rock and roll, the Ford Thunderbird and Chevrolet Corvette cars, Herman

Miller chairs, the Hula Hoop and frisbee, J.D Salinger's *Catcher In The Rye*, Frank Lloyd Wright's design for the Guggenheim Museum, women's two-piece suits and the Aloha shirt, for example. All have become iconic. What made these items special was their attribute of being "cool" (as in beatnik lingo) and functional in and of themselves. If there was an aesthetic, it was accidental and fueled by the buoyancy of the post-World War II era.

Everything mentioned above still exists or is in production, albeit in an updated form. Fender and Gibson now charge extra for faithful recreations of their original designs. American cars are more reliable than ever but are no longer in the same league style-wise as their European counterparts like Jaguar, BMW, Ferrari and Volvo. I own a 1970 Land Rover that is the epitome of practicalness which has, paradoxically, become a thing of beauty due to its rugged simplicity. Around one million copies of *Catcher In The Rye* are still sold a year. And the Guggenheim Museum has become a landmark in architecture, partially due to how it mimics the shape of a nautilus shell. Any good design will contain a timeless quality that never goes out of fashion.

Most of these enduring items have a functionality about them whether it be an electric pickup attached to a slab of wood, literature that is a touchstone for teenage rebellion or some molded plastic that can be used for fun or as a chair. At some point in time, the marriage of style and function separated when things and trends became more and more disposable. In William McDonough's book *Cradle To Cradle*, he points out a history of poor design since the Industrial Revolution that has created the by-products of pollution, additional landfills and unnecessary waste of materials that could have been reused. On the other hand, who wants to throw away a Nambé bowl or a Hudson Bay blanket?

What has happened to beauty in America? Well, if it doesn't need to exist in either politics, economics or occasionally popular culture, what's the point? It's telling that one of the most celebrated categories in book sales at the moment is dystopian fiction. Perhaps that is a reflection of how some no longer believe in even the possibility of uplifting aesthetics. When I listen to contemporary music, there is a noticeable absence of harmonic and rhythmic complexity. The lack of strong musically lyrical content may exemplify the lack of harmony within our society. The rhythmic and electronic drive of rap and hip-hop illustrates the focus on the pulse of contemporary culture at the expense of poetic language and melody. Hollywood and television have always been preoccupied with what sells—particularly sex and violence. But sensuality is more often found in European films like *I Am Love* and *The English Patient*.

If I was to name a cause of this loss of "aesthetic enrichment," it would be a market economy that is very good at responding to and focussing on where a profit can be made. Beauty has no reliance on anything external in order to be created. It is in itself a precious value that nourishes and enriches the soul. An argument could be made that our educational system is far more concerned with training future participants in that market economy than with recognizing the existence and need for the soul to thrive. A happy human may not necessarily be a productive one but they definitely won't be causing harm to themselves, others or the planet. While crime is currently in recession in America, public shootings of innocent people are on the rise. One often can't find beauty if they feel disenfranchised, impoverished and hopeless.

Maybe we are looking from the wrong direction in terms of obsessively fueling a capitalist culture. Instead, teaching an appreciation of aesthetics, which usually expands through creativity, would enrich the individual while creating a society not based on money and its dark sides of theft and inequality but on beauty and, with it, a shift back to a true democracy. Bring poetry to elementary schools, let every child have a chance to create with their hands, allow kids to play freely again without necessarily a screen or adult involved, visit the Grand Canyon, dance to live music regardless of your age, read to each other, support local art organizations, write your partner a poem and, most importantly, seek and create beauty incessantly, knowing your life depends on it.

The Fall of Jazz

I've been a part-time jazz DJ for forty years and have watched the listening audience get smaller and smaller. During the Jazz Age in the 1920s and 1930s, the music was the primary genre for dancing. This stretched into the 1940s with the big bands and the songs that my parents fell in love to. Once the size of the groups shrank and went from the dance halls to the clubs, jazz took a back seat to the new kid on the block, rock and roll. In other words, jazz went from being received by the body to listening with the head. Dave Brubeck made it on to the cover of TIME magazine in November of 1954. After that, it became hip music with more focus on individual players like Miles Davis, John Coltrane and Thelonious Monk, for instance, with their technical prowess and compositional genius. The best-selling jazz album of all time is Miles Davis's *Kind of Blue* that included (Col)Trane, Cannonball Adderley, Bill Evans, Paul Chambers and Jimmy Cobb. This is exactly where jazz radio got stuck and is still in a holding pattern.

Some believe that jazz is America's classical music. This shouldn't mean that it has to become a museum piece. Sure, it's still thriving at colleges, universities and music schools but the clubs have become few and far between with cover charges that are beyond the reach of most people. Record and CD purchases are barely over 1 percent of total sales. Times and tastes change and every generation wants to have their own music to define personal identity. Jazz, like blues, has become out of fashion. The guitarist John Scofield once said that jazz is America's fastest dying art form.

This brings me to jazz DJs in particular. If you are over fifty and doing a regular show, you are probably playing mainstream music in the vein of *Kind of Blue* or Charlie Parker. It's all great art but not doing a thing to attract a new and perhaps a younger audience. Why? Because only the music of dead people is being played which is wonderful for those who grew up during that time but not particularly alive for someone who didn't unless it's an academic exercise. Related to this is the very old habit from over fifty years ago of announcing the names of all of the players to a particular piece of music. Regardless of age, if one is tuning in for the first time, you might as well be reading the obituary column of a group of strangers. Is there any other music genre today where this is done? No. The pleasure of jazz is not about academia or trivia but in hearing great music. At least two-thirds of a show should be devoted to players that are still with us and recording.

Now down to the nitty-gritty. Jazz is an improvisational art form. I have heard and know of DJs who create set lists in advance of their respective shows. How does anyone know their feelings or thoughts hours prior to an event? Being stuck in your head isn't particularly useful when it comes to art. It seems to me that the programmer should imitate the improvisational model when it comes to selecting music. As much as jazz radio loves *Kind of Blue*, didn't anyone read the liner notes by Bill Evans? Whether one is using CDs, vinyl or Spotify, there is a song-by-song process in building a set that can only be done in the moment and on the fly. A real skill exists here that, for the most part, has become a lost art in contemporary radio. I attribute it to the advent of the iPod and its random shuffling of music. The problem is that there is no flow from one song to the next. It's bad enough that I'll dive across a room to change the station. Jazz is already on thin ice then when a DJ puts a Nina Simone song next to, say, something by Fela Kuti (this did happen); the beautiful Ferrari you're driving along the Italian coast has just missed the turn and is tumbling towards the rocks at the bottom of the cliff. That's how you lose an audience.

I worked with a DJ in Colorado years ago who had notebooks filled with segues of popular music that he had accidentally discovered over the course of his career. Some were songs that had the same key musically, some with the same instrumentation and some that had a similar feel. His approach taught me a lot about what I could do within the realm of jazz. Now I've taken it one step further by adding poetry to my shows and seeing how to make the feel of a poem flow into the music that follows. By the way, reading poetry over a bed of music was fine fifty years ago; however, it now feels like tearing my body into two parts. A good poem doesn't need the feel and rhythm of music to bring it about. A good poem already has its own feel and rhythm that doesn't need to be distracted by adding something else.

My love of music began with folk then gravitated towards jazz due to its harmonic and rhythmic complexity. And it was the genre that spoke to my inner world of feeling and sensation. Hearing John Coltrane's version of "My Favorite Things" for the first time was evidence of something I unconsciously knew—that creativity was freedom and the physical, emotional and spiritual universe is, in fact, infinite. Trane was pushing the outer limits while Evan's version of "My Foolish Heart" went just as far internally. These were revelations that opened up a world of possibilities unknown to me before. This is what can be achieved for the listener every week during a show. It is up to us older DJs and jazz lovers to figure out a way to attract a new audience. Jazz doesn't need to be yet another endangered species.

Reading Poems Out Loud

I've been a radio DJ since the early 1970s when I delved into the world of low-watt transmission at St. Lawrence University. After graduation, I took a small break to make a living and split many cords of wood by hand in Vermont. A few years later, I moved to Colorado and was back in a control room, playing jazz exclusively once a week. Later, at another station in the same valley, I began to add poetry on Valentine's Day. That was about forty years ago. I'm now a DJ in northern New Mexico and, instead of on occasional poetry, I combine jazz with poetry under the umbrella of a theme each week. Those topics can cover everything from holidays to worldly or internal matters like nurturing the soul and finding balance. If I'm guessing correctly, I've read almost a thousand poems on the air during this last stretch.

Whether that number makes me any good at what I do is up to the listener. Juggling the three elements of music, poetry and theme is never certain in terms of the outcome.

I strive to have everything flow together while doing what I can to remain transparent. I want the art to dominate, not my personality. This is quite contrary to most radio stations that want a human personality on the air. For me, art is all that's needed.

When it comes to reading poetry, I realized a number of things a few years ago. Poems are not widely read, in general, beyond classrooms, workshops, the sofas of lovers of language and, of course, readings. Unlike other art forms, there is no actual standard that one can refer to as far as how a poem should sound when read out loud. One can easily go online today and hear lots of great poets since the beginning of live recording with varying results. Often, I'm struck by how unpoetic a reading can be as if the author was pronouncing or declaring something rather than reciting a poem. So when I started reading on the air, I had no example to follow—just my instincts and intuition. This may have been a good thing as far as finding my own way.

Being a poetry DJ is no different than choosing music—a background is helpful so that a sensibility can be created. I double majored in English and music for no real conscious reason beyond my love for language and already being a musician. In retrospect, it was the perfect background for a future completely unknown to me. One of my college professors, Albert Glover, was a Black Mountain School poet who had Charles Olson as a mentor. Little did I know at the time how hip this would be for a new college student in the post 1960s.

At the time, Dr. Glover was also working on a chapbook project with other Black Mountain School poets based on Olson's poem "A Plan for a Curriculum of the Soul." Contemporary poetry was now in my hands. This was my first big step away from the confines of rhyme and meter that had dominated the form until the modern poets. That old paradigm had created a legion of spoken-word readers who insisted on a singsong method of recitation that often sounded like a parent trying to croon a nursery rhyme to a child. Unfortunately, it still lingers today with usually poor results.

So there I was around 1980 reading the love poems of Pablo Neruda, Yevgeny Yevtushenko and Anselm Hollo (another Black Mountain poet) on the air from my own collection. This was before the popularization of the Internet which completely opened up access to poems without the need to buy more books. I still possess a library of contemporary poets because I'd rather have the tactile experience of a book in my hands than look at a screen. I've gone from Ovid (back in college) to Larry Levis, Marie Howe, Tony Hoagland and Naomi Shihab Nye, among so many others. My sensibility keeps getting formed, shaped and refined so that I can, hopefully, select good poetry. That discernment is essential if I'm going to do a public reading.

The difference between writing a poem and reading the same out loud is the difference between creation and performance. This is an important distinction. Since the 1960s, we've grown to love the singer/songwriter by feeling that the original is always the best version. Then Jimi Hendrix came along with his cover of Dylan's "All Along The Watchtower" as everything was changing and becoming electric in a new way. This followed the path of improvisation found in the world of jazz. For me, that familiar path is the key to what I'm doing when I read on the air. It's gotten to the point that I no longer have to think about it. Like the musician creating a solo, it's more about feeling into a poem and its internal rhythm, measuring the words, putting emphasis where necessary, even changing the tone of the voice as needed so that the listener might be drawn in—not just to the poem itself, but into the poet's particular sensibility.

On one level, I want my voice to sound intimately conversational, like talking to a dear friend. There's an openness that has to happen towards both the poem itself and the listener. It's this approach that allows the possibility of getting inside the poem. If I can't understand, absorb and take on that sensibility, I certainly can't speak it. This happens with readers who don't vary the tone of their voice, quietly lecture through repetition of particular lines, overemphasize certain phrases or, aren't comfortable with public speaking. All of that is even before the work of improvising to find the melody, rhythm and tone of a piece as a reader speaks. A great or celebrity voice isn't enough and can be a distraction away from the work of art. Poetry has never been interested in celebrity. Like any piece of art, some sort of frame is needed to separate the work from ordinary life. In the case of poetry, that frame is silence before and after a poem. Entering and leaving another world needs the space to do so.

In some sense, I realize that I'm asking for the impossible. How do I, on one hand, remain transparent, while on the other, become fully present to the writing itself? This process is more than just trying on clothes; it's an attempt to live and breathe the poem for the duration of the reading. I'll be honest. Sometimes it works and sometimes it doesn't. When it does, I'm either trembling or about to cry. This is what it's come to after forty years. I was hoping to ignite some love between listeners during that first Valentine's Day show. It is still my hope. But in order to make that happen, I discovered that I needed to learn how to fall in love first with the poem itself.

A Case Against the Use of Recreational Marijuana

As of this writing, seventeen states and the District of Columbia have legalized the use of marijuana recreationally. Medical use is endorsed by thirty-six states along with D.C., Guam, Puerto Rico and the United States Virgin Islands. Clearly, we are in a trend that is moving forward with more and more pot use. In the process, cannabis is becoming just another product to be marketed, sold and consumed for profit like any other in our capitalist culture.

It wasn't until college that I tried pot during my freshman year. I was listening to a Joni Mitchell album and, as the high kicked in, I wondered why the song being played was lasting so long. I already had a strong emotional connection to this music but felt like I couldn't get close to those familiar feelings under the influence. While I enjoyed the altering of ordinary consciousness, to be cut loose from the anchor of my emotional body was completely disorientating. It was like a weird version of my childhood where my feelings never had a place within my family. In retrospect, how I felt emotionally became the most reliable version of an inner home I could create.

The idea of spending money on drugs made no sense to me so I only used occasionally. In other words, it was no big deal. Towards the end of college, I remember growing some pot beneath some electric power lines near a house I was renting. That particular strain of pot just created an experience of being heavy and sluggish. Then the 1980s came along with the prevailing trend of cocaine use. Alcohol and pot were perfect antidotes to the energy surge of coke. We used to mix marijuana and magic mushrooms together in a pipe to smoke before going skiing. The 'shrooms gave a lift to counteract the dulling down of the pot.

A few years later, my son was born and the days of drug use were over. I knew the moment he entered this world that everything had changed. To keep up with his glorious, innocent presence, I had to be equally present. There were already a few other signs prior to his birth that had me weaning off drugs. One was that I was losing touch with my own creativity as a musician by not practicing and learning new material. Getting stoned made me lazy. The other took place during a conversation with a friend who wanted to talk about his occupation, tile setting. We were high as the sky and to talk about something mundane was like walking straight into hell. Yet getting high prevented an enduring focus needed to talk about deeper things.

That was over thirty-five years ago and I haven't used anything since except for the rare, occasional drink. Living in northern New Mexico, I've discovered that marijuana use has a history here that surpasses the 1960s and the hippie generation. I certainly know some pot users but no one who I hang out with. When coming home at night from a film, I can tell who has been drinking and who has been smoking dope by their driving habits. The drinkers weave and the smokers go *real* slow. I just keep my distance. The interesting thing is that drug use here is as ordinary as buying groceries. There isn't much judgment unless someone's life is a stake.

I've read the pro and con arguments regarding marijuana. I find no one who is talking about the effects that cannot be easily measured. First and foremost, drugs are powerful energies that can be used beneficially or to the detriment of our well-being. Medical cannabis is still in the early stages of study and has shown some promise in the alleviation of pain and nausea. What troubles me is what I noticed back in my twenties: that part of getting high included the separation from the emotional body. For pain relief, it's great. For being fully present, it's not. Without our feeling sense of the world, we have immediately cut our perceptual awareness significantly. A friend has another way to look at this by asking, "Why put holes in your aura?"

This plays in beautifully with our culture that is alive mostly from the neck up and rewards those who make a living that way accordingly. The more degrees and training one has, the more one will likely get paid. The result is that we are becoming more and more of a mental society with stress and depression on the rise. Per capita, the United States is the number one country on the planet in terms of antidepressant use. The suicide rate in America has increased by 25 percent since 1999. Technology, as wonderful as it can be, is playing a strong hand in keeping us in our heads. The casualties are the individual emotional landscapes and inner lives which are no longer in balance with what's going on with our brains. The push for the availability of recreational pot may not be so much about having fun, as it used to be, but about checking out.

Dropping down the rabbit hole further, the loss of emotional information has an indelible impact on our intuitive and instinctual perceptions. Without those, we never would have survived as a species—much less made the leap to build or live in cities. Humans would have been just another extinct species killed off by predators. A loss of grounded decision-making can be seen in the effects of long-term use where short and long-term memory has been diminished, creating the sense that some wiring has been fried since emotional, intuitive and instinctual attention hasn't been used in so long.

There's been a curious and subtle shift from what were once considered our freedoms to renaming them as our rights. Freedom takes work while a right wants to be defended. Legalizing and marketing marijuana as an easy way to pursue happiness sounds like freedom when, in fact, it's about the right to check out. Maybe that's what the times call for when so little good news prevails. And maybe it's time to check back in to becoming fully human again which would be the best news of all and the surest way to deal with the state of the world.

Treading the Waters of Spirituality

I don't believe in a spiritual path any more than in a bird or a fish who maps out all of its wanderings in advance. I also don't believe in the unassailability of spirituality any more than the pretension of a pedophile priest. Just by saying "spiritual" in some contexts, one can allege to be immune to criticism and reproach. It's the hope of light without shadow. It's all sky without the gravity of the deep dark earth forever shifting beneath our feet.

Annie Dillard wrote in *For The Time Being,* "'Spiritual Path' is the hilarious popular term for those night-blind mesas and flayed hills in which people grope, for decades on end, with the goal of knowing the absolute." The problem is that a path implies a linear progression from the depths upward rather than simply exploring through wandering. Supporting this is the idea that a person can pay the fees or be educated into spirituality through workshops, retreats, a meditation practice, religion, whatever. As a result, a whole industry has been created with the same underlying belief as everyday advertising—that none of us will ever be good enough without some sort of help or by consuming more things and experiences. The self-help world is on the same trajectory, with perfection as the goal which is a version of "knowing the absolute." Do I really have to be perfect to have a feeling towards the Divine?

"Meister Eckhart radically revises the whole notion of spiritual programs. He says that there is no such thing as a spiritual journey. If a little shocking, this is refreshing. If there were a spiritual journey, it would be only a quarter inch long, though many miles deep" (John O'Donohue, *Anam Cara*). It's like sensing into a dream upon waking, by diving into the waters in the hope of coming up with a pearl. Is that pearl an indication of forward motion, a seductive detour or a reminder about my own wisdom? To what extent are any of us willing to delve into our depths at any moment? Is it in the silence of those depths where we can find the sacred?

In this sense, a spiritual path implies that our identities and egos can be brought forward with enough guidance. Like most self-help, there is no acknowledgment for the existence of the unconscious or the soul. Once you add the element of the unknown, the path vanishes. It is easy looking back on my life to notice a passage through the turmoil of my father's rigidity, sibling competition, my escape to college, codependence, my son's birth, my business and then hitting the wall when all I believed crumbled. I was just doing what I thought was expected of me. Or was my soul orchestrating these random experiences so that I could finally come home to the holiness of myself?

Around the age of seven, my son used to say, "That's

how you *don't* do it." Pure wisdom. Of course, he was talking about something functional but there is a defining quality about a path which belies the difficulty and subtlety of coming to terms with our anger and grief as well as expressing our compassion and forgiveness, for instance. I'm still working with, not on, these places inside of me for no particular goal outside of not liking the feeling of being stuck. And I know that whatever I don't resolve inside will show up as an external situation in my day-to-day life or as body symptom later on. Either way, I have to do the work.

Is there a progression towards understanding and having a relationship with God? I don't know. I used to believe, like many, that if I prayed enough and tried to be a good person, my prayers might get answered. That ultimately felt like a system run by a puritanical god. Then I started to find glimpses of another approach in the poetry of Hafiz and especially of Rilke. Rilke's poem, "Give Me Your Hand" was one of the most reassuring. Here's my translation:

> *God speaks to each one of us as we're created*
> *then goes in silence with us from the night.*
> *As if through a cloud,*
> *these are the words we faintly hear.*
>
> *'Sent out by your senses,*
> *go to your longing's edge,*
> *give me clothes.*
> *Burn like fire bringing shadows*
>
> *that cover me completely.*
> *Let it all happen to you: beauty and terror.*
> *You must go on. No feeling is too far.*

Do not separate yourself from me.

Close to here is the country called Life.
You will know you have entered
by its seriousness.

Give me your hand.'

    Even with the presence of my parents, siblings, teachers, friends and lovers, there can be a loneliness, or a solitude that arises. That solitude is a refuge. My loneliness is a feeling of being stranded far from the world and perhaps even the divine. Crowds can be the most difficult with so many people and so little connection. "You must go on." When I let the loneliness exhaust itself, a calm arises. That calm is a deep knowing that I am not completely alone because there are always the endless sky and earth to hold my feet, the water of my blood and my temporal breath.

    For me, it's about being fully alive. Give me the blues so I can learn compassion. Give me some music so I can dance. Give me some windows into what my deepest self wants and I'll oblige. What I've discovered is this—that growing into a soul by directing my loving towards the challenging trials of living is the most difficult and glorious work of all.

Victim Empathy

(Written for the State of Colorado Restorative Justice Program)

To empathize with someone is to place yourself in their shoes. This is more than simulating a physical act. It is something that takes emotional and psychological understanding. Within the concept is using the tools of compassion and imagination. Without mercy towards another, anything can be rationalized. If I can't feel what it is like to be harmed in some fashion, that lack of emotional intelligence will increase the chances that I will harm another. To act without imagining the consequences to another person, a family or the world around us is to behave without a moral compass. Without some sort of guide, we can lose our way.

For those incarcerated, this is not new information. Instead, an inward perspective might be considered. Here's the secret that you will never hear on the evening news: *everyone* is looking for redemption. It doesn't matter if you are in a state prison, in the prison of a nine-to-five job that you hate, the solitary confinement of a relationship that is abusive or trapped in the cultural beliefs of monetary success and approval—redemption is longing for discovery. We all want to be redeemed in order to find whatever resonates with our deepest selves, whether that be a form of happiness, peace of mind, a healthy body or connection to another, for instance. With deliverance as a path, the map becomes clearer. It also brings in the possibility of help from a higher power if you are spiritually inclined.

So where does one begin? Unraveling the past so that some understanding can be reached is one way. This is where pieces can be found that might have caused certain behaviors to take place. Many of our adult actions are formed unconsciously by parental example. Take a mother and father who are violent towards each other. Violence will probably be tolerated, maybe acted upon, in the child's mind and life. Or if the parents were never present, the son or daughter might have had to survive on the streets where the rules are very different than consensual reality. Acknowledging how we were influenced is important for the possibility of individual change that opens the door to empathy. Without that knowing, a cycle of shame, blame and rationalizations can go on forever. We can't change how we were influenced, but we can alter what we decided about ourselves due to those situations.

Another way to look at this is by taking an internal inventory to see what does and doesn't come from love. Whatever doesn't, usually a belief that led to poor results, can be changed with some work. That includes identification of the belief and acknowledgement of the adverse consequences. Here is where self-forgiveness can be a valuable tool. There are some options to help with this work. Create a statement that begins with "I forgive myself for believing..." For example, "I forgive myself for believing that stealing causes no harm." Or "I forgive myself for judging myself as worthless and unlovable." You are forgiving yourself for believing or judging something. Saying these out loud or putting them in writing can add to their power. Another option is the generic statement, "I'm sorry, forgive me, thank you, I love you." The explanation behind this is "I'm sorry" for whatever I, my family, my ancestors or my genetic line did to create this situation; "forgive me" for my actions; "thank you" for mirroring back to me what I still need to forgive within; and "I love you" to your basic self. I use this statement silently every day all of the time. What is being asked of the user is to take full responsibility for whatever happens in their life. This may be a big leap so decide what works for you.

Self-forgiveness is a powerful tool among many that helps keep things clean emotionally, psychologically and spiritually. That is where the rubber meets the road leading to redemption. Addressing the past paves the way for keeping current with the present. Within our previous actions, there is always the question whether anyone has been harmed. Here is where the deeper work begins. If I can't find compassion for myself, even in my worst moments, then I'll never find compassion for another. Knowing a situation is one thing, understanding it is another. My father raised my siblings and me with the phrase, "No ifs, ands, or buts." This caused incredible resentment and anger inside of me for years until I realized that this was how he was raised by his German father. His own fear of authority short-circuited any possibility of curiosity about alternatives to raising children. Understanding this gave me a foothold in empathizing with his childhood. Then my imagination kicked in as I grasped how my grandfather had helped create my emotionally unavailable father. I was further helped with this understanding by learning that his generation did not value emotional availability in men. All of this paved the way for me to develop compassion and forgiveness towards my father.

Was I a victim? Not consciously. Identifying exclusively as a victim is disempowering. Yet there are those who are the injured parties of crime and other thoughtless actions. Does that make them a victim forever? This is a matter that can only be decided personally. Wounds to the soul may or may not be forgivable, depending on the individual. Let's assume that someone was impacted on a deep level. If you were the perpetrator, are you willing to acknowledge this wound caused by your actions? Working with your own wounds is the ground for understanding how someone else might have been harmed. It's the first step. It includes using the strength of courage, humility, patience and surrender. Without those, you won't get very far.

Next, there is deciding what action to take on that road to redemption. Now we come to the idea of amends work. There are many versions of this including restorative justice (meeting and talking with a victim), prayer, forgiveness, maybe even some form of correspondence—basically any process that neutralizes a situation. Empathizing with a victim is the first step to making amends. For a moment, imagine that this victim was your closest friend, brother or sister. How do you feel now? How would you feel if the crime committed happened to you? There may be some guilt, anger or humiliation. All of those feelings are repercussions of being vulnerable. This is where redemption takes place. When you can tap into the vulnerability someone felt when being injured, you are empathizing. It's what makes us magnificently human—when we can touch one another through being fragile. A perpetrator who has felt what it's like to be a victim will be redeemed through transformation and the possibility of peace of mind.

One last note—that kind of tenderness is rarely, if ever, tolerated in the course of incarceration. So be agile in its selective use. This is sacred terrain which should never be shared casually.

Moral Authority

I recently came across the notion of "six grounding virtues" on a website which got me thinking about the idea of moral authority and who, if anyone, can make such pronouncements anymore. Are the seven heavenly virtues no longer relevant or grounding? Those include chastity, temperance, charity, diligence, patience, kindness and humility as the opposites of the seven capital sins of lust, gluttony, greed, sloth, wrath, envy and pride. It was the Catholic Church that created these lists as a roadmap in how to navigate life and be free of sin.

Of course, that church has lost its own ability to pronounce anything as far as how we should live due to the ongoing sexual scandals and lack of transparency by its own clergy. Other religions are suffering as well. The amount of violence perpetuated by certain Muslims towards others from Indonesia to the Middle East never seems to end. The tarnishing of the Jewish religion by Israel in its violence towards Palestinians is another example. India is now ranked fourth in the world for religious intolerance resulting in harm caused to Muslims. Evangelicals in the United States haven't fared much better in their psychological violence against anyone with an alternative sexual orientation. The only large spiritual group left that has mostly stayed true to itself seems to be the Buddhists.

Other places where we have looked for guidance and integrity have been in government, education, law enforcement and medicine. Sadly, as much as we have relied on those institutions, they too have fallen prey to their own failings of judgment and character. As the violations of trust keep getting uncovered, a moral vacuum has been created which is being filled by anyone with a platform, allowing them to make a public assertion regardless of its validity. That loss of trust has placed us in a precarious transition where bearings are no longer external but deep inside.

Regarding the "six grounding virtues" website, the first virtue is "Words That Matter." Matter to who? Virtues are not subjective like language but are aspects of our higher selves that exist within everyone. The problem is not words that matter but a failure to honor imagination—the foundation for all language—that our current culture perpetuates. This can be seen in the slashing of art programs in early education, the exclusion of poetry in general and PhDs primarily trained to be only in their heads through linear thinking. Without imagination, we can't sympathize, empathize or be curious enough to create connection. And without connection, who are we talking to?

Related to this is the fifth virtue offered, "Generous Listening." In a world that insists on fracturing our attention through sound bites, commercials, Twitter feeds and breaking news, deep listening is as much a fantasy as getting your neighbor to tell you their dreams from the night before. If there is little in our world that promotes listening to ourselves, how could anyone truly listen to someone else?

Yes, civility has taken a huge hit—especially in the world of politics. But how does "Adventurous Civility" (number three on the virtue list) really differ from kindness? Buzz phrases are like fast food in their lack of nutrition. The list goes on with "Humility" and "Patience" which are part of the Catholic list. Finally, "Hospitality" is listed which seems more like a colloquial version of charity. So I'm left with the relevance of the original list and the lack of originality and value in the updated version. Which implies the question, Has human behavior changed significantly in any way over the past centuries? The crumbling of those institutions that once offered moral authority probably best answers that question.

A vacuum created wants to pull anything in to fill the void. This is where true patience is needed; not to artificially fill that space but to allow for something new to be created instead. Perhaps this transition is calling upon us to discover another way, first individually then collectively. The diligence to practice charity towards chaos during such a process of creation is also a path. As is the temperance of not having to fix what appears to be broken. I look towards and get hints from those who walk the walk so to speak. There are many who include Mother Theresa, Martin Luther King, Jr., Father Gregory Boyle and Pema Chödrön, for instance. They are Roman Catholic, Protestant, Jesuit and Buddhist respectively. In other words, a spiritual aspect was, or is very much a part of their lives. Virtues without some sort of spirituality are just talk.

Conversation is a good beginning. But it's not enough. The striving for a virtuous life has to be put on the playing field of everyday living which inevitably implies the risk of success as well as failure. This takes place first and foremost *internally*. The idea that one has lived a life of such contemplation to believe that they have new virtues to offer is presumptuous. But then to describe these new things without any mention whatsoever of inner work, as if the external impacts are the only concern, is new age folly.

Inner work is grounding work which by necessity is practiced in the world. Only after facing inward to tame the dragons of addiction, prejudice, false beliefs and anything else that prevents us from becoming whole can we become truly grounded to possibly inhabit virtues. This first work is the key. If I don't know how to be charitable to myself, how can I be authentically charitable to others? This applies to all of the original virtues. No, we don't need a new list. What we need are those who are willing to do the difficult soul work that opens the gates to the possibility of living morally and ethically. If that work has been done, true humility would show that no one, myself included, is in a position to claim moral authority over anyone except oneself—especially in these times.

Living, Not Meaning

While I was growing up, my father would usually end a one-on-one discussion with the words, "I just want you to be happy." What that really meant was that he wanted me to follow his advice about making a living along with the warnings and condemnations about my inclinations towards the arts. From a kind eye, he was doing what he thought a father should do as it replicated what his father did and his father's father probably going back for generations. Artistic aspirations are not a trait that belongs to a family of engineers, farmers, sea captains and executives that are first and foremost pragmatic. Undoing the clasp of expectations often involves creating new territory.

The idea of my happiness seemed to give meaning to my father in terms of being a parent. What was taking place had nothing to do with me being happy but with his happiness in the idea that he didn't have to worry about me financially if I had a reliable profession. This became obvious once I was a successful property manager. "You need to get a real estate license," became his new advice for me to become happy. This was what my father could understand. As with many of his peers, the impossible challenge was how to be a parent of children growing up through the 1950s and 1960s. His own meaning was found in the relationship with my mother. That kind of love needs no explanation.

I have a friend who once talked about the importance of knowing why we are here. In other words, the meaning of life. I recall telling him that meaning is a mental exercise which doesn't integrate with the rest of who we are. The emotional body just wants to feel, the physical body wants to move (or rest), the psychological body is forever examining—holding on to and replacing belief—while the spiritual body wants a connection to those larger energies some call God, Allah, Jehovah, Krishna, Buddha, Christ or The Great Spirit. In other words, meaning holds no value in my heart, my gut and in how I pray. Psychologically, we could pretend that the significance of our lives through success, awards, degrees, even friendships, holds some truth—until it doesn't.

That's the problem, isn't it? Meaning is just a thought that may or may not be true depending on your current reference point or belief system which is usually in flux. None of us know who or what will still be here from one moment to the next. Many of the things I believed in my twenties no longer work.

> *People say that what we're all seeking is a meaning for life. I don't think that's what we're really seeking. I think that what we're seeking is an experience of being alive, so that our life experiences on the purely physical plane will have resonances with our own innermost being and reality, so that we actually feel the rapture of being alive.*
>
> — Joseph Campbell, *The Power of Myth*

Those who keep talking about meaning never appear to be experiencing "the rapture of being alive." I've become wary of others who are frequently talking about meaning, which is like a dog chasing its own tail. Did my father's advice make him a bad parent? No, not at all. What I discovered was that his best lessons were those that he did without showing any intentional guidance, like going to work day in and day out, being faithful to my mother and doing his best to show us places he loved. It was what he loved that gave me the best memory snapshots. In that sense, his purpose was a lighthouse beacon in the night.

As a musician, I can talk about what a particular song might mean (though I rarely do). Music is only one of many doors to a wide-open field of possibilities that, like nature, continually changes from one moment to the next. How will that song feel at a wedding or a funeral of a friend? Only until I sing the words at that particular event will I know. The rest is improvisation based on experience.

Which brings up the other problem with the quest to explain one's life. A fixed outcome of meaning defies the nature of reality, from the regeneration of the cells in our bodies every seven years to the continually changing weather. One could get broad and claim that love is what life is all about. But there are thousands of ways to express that. What does love mean? Who cares? I just know how it feels which is more than enough for me. Does my life have a point? No more than that dog chasing its tail. For me, I love when my body is in motion (especially through dancing or swimming); when I'm creating with words, music or photos; when I'm connecting to another person beyond small talk; when I'm in the presence of good art via poetry, film or live music; and when I can feel "the rapture of being alive." I've now lived two-thirds of a century and have yet to hear anyone confess that they have discovered the meaning of life. Have you? To quote Joseph Campbell again, "Life has no meaning. Each of us has meaning and we bring it to life. It is a waste to be asking the question when you are the answer."

My Fate

I've had a love affair with the earth ever since I was a child. Like most kids of my generation, free time was spent not with technology but in the woods. Are baby boomers the last to have experienced this pleasure? In a sense, I was more at home in nature where there were no judgments, demands or expectations. It is still a refuge for me today, even though my own home is filled with over forty plants including tropicals such as hibiscus, plumeria, anthurium and banana. Other plants include cactus orchid, euphorbia, Christmas cactus, Cape primrose and philodendron which are all more suited to the high desert where I live. A lemon tree is now in bloom and its flowers produce a scent that might be described as tropical honeysuckle.

Once I began air travel, my seating choice has always been the same—next to the window. My love of the earth could then be expanded from the ground view to seeing everything from the New York skyline with the nearby Statue of Liberty to the cloud shrouded peaks of Mauna Kea and Mauna Loa on the Big Island of Hawaii. And how thrilling it was once when a pilot lowered the plane so all could see the

Yosemite valley with El Capitan as we rolled slightly from left to right to take in the view. On a recent trip back east, I took in Lake Erie, Buffalo and all of the Finger Lakes of New York as I was heading to Albany.

It was during this trip on my return flight that I got a glimpse of Englewood, New Jersey where I was born. This was after already visiting the house where I grew up in the Hudson Valley, the paint on the clapboard siding peeling, the huge silver maple tree on the front lawn where we used to climb now long gone and the neighborhood still much the same—middle-class and deteriorating. Only the number of leaves on that maple could compete with the wealth of memories. This drive-by was just after a trip to the Motor Vehicle Department where my then ninety-three-year-old mother was renewing her driver's license (Will it be her last?). That same location was where I got my first learner's permit and subsequent license.

Curiously, I had forgotten about the subterranean office across the street where I used to have weekly visits to an ear, nose and throat specialist when I was ten due to a case of swimmer's ear. In the summers, I swam almost every day which created an inner ear infection and two holes in the ear drum. That doctor once threatened to hit me when I refused to have a rubber hose inserted many inches up one nostril. He had done this procedure before, causing me pain like I've never experienced. Every Wednesday afternoon, my mother would pick me up from school and I would go with dread down those stairs to the doctor's office knowing that there was only agony ahead.

So there I was sitting alone at the Motor Vehicle Department, hard benches like church pews, my mother inside having an eye test while I was looking at the descending entrance to a childhood hell. The doctor has since passed away and the office space looks like it has been converted to a living area for the home above. Even with the charge of memory, that entrance had a complete neutrality about it. Take away the characters of a play and all that is left is the stage. Without the office sign, the patients going in and out and the empty parking lot, those stairs had become just another architectural feature.

It was this neutrality inside that caught me by surprise. I have always identified with the pieces of my past, good and bad, as if I couldn't exist without their story. Yet somehow my old identities connected to where I was born, where I grew up and where I saw the compassionless doctor no longer had a hold on me. Following the license renewal, my mother and I visited Lake Mohonk where we used to spend a few weeks each summer. Again, a tidal wave of memory. The garden area had twenty thousand tulips in bloom at that moment. Those flowers could have been a scrapbook of our experiences—vibrant, varietal yet dispersed. There I was, camera in hand, a photo heaven, documenting the moment while knowing on some level that I, too, was just a fleeting guest. There was that neutrality again but without the length of distance. It was immediate, palpable and unexpectedly delicious.

Yesterday, I received a phone call from someone in my high school graduating class letting me know about an upcoming fiftieth reunion. This was about a month after trying on the linen pants I wore to the wedding of my long defunct marriage. They still fit! That summer had me back playing publicly in an electric blues band like I first did in college. The poet, Wendell Berry, finished his poem "Manifesto: The

Mad Farmer Liberation Front," with the words "Practice resurrection." Quite accidentally, this seems to be what has been happening. Yes, the Englewood hospital is where I happened to be born to two particular parents. The Hudson Valley is where I grew up. The western United States is where I've been living as an adult. It's all precious and specific to me while, at the same time, ambivalent and casual. My life could have been different. This detachment has become a blossoming delight that can balance the passion of a moment. I don't want to forsake one for the other.

Training

Their bodily exercises, too, were less rigorous during their campaigns, and [they] were allowed a regimen less rigid. They were the only men in the world for whom war brought a respite in the training for war.
— Plutarch on the Spartans

Never give a sword to a man who can't dance.
— Confucius

Like their neighbors to the north in Athens, ancient Sparta was known for its ability to thrive through austerity and battle but not for any real contributions to the arts, philosophy or culture in general. What was missing? A fuller sense of humanity. Hence, the second quote above contains the wisdom that someone should not be armed without first discovering their own humanness. But I do like one part of the Spartan way—that continual training, though not for war, is the path. Let me explain.

From the perspective of the soul, the first work is always inside. This puts the responsibility of our lives, for the most part, in our own hands. Immediately, shame and blame are taken off the table. How? Shaming and blaming externalize your world often by projecting what hasn't been resolved inside. It's the easy way of not taking responsibility for our participation in the dance of life. Since very few of us are taught to look inward, some retraining usually needs to take place. This can be a challenge with a culture that thrives on the goals of financial profit rather than personal responsibility. However, once this new view is in place, the field of possibilities fully opens.

There are a number of ways to walk there. Looking inwards, consider the physical, emotional, mental/psychological and spiritual areas of your life. How are you at training and maintaining these four dimensions? When was the last time you evaluated your diet, your exercise routine, your beliefs, your relationship to your higher self and your compassion, forgiveness and patience? When was the last time you laughed, cried, got angry, sang or danced? What you are training for, regardless of age, is your fullest potential.

To use the Plutarch quote above as a metaphor, this ongoing work is what puts you into the best possible shape to confront the difficulties of living. Keeping in shape and in tune with yourself is the work. The world will always give you pop quizzes to see how well you have trained. Yes, there are some basic tools to help with this process. I've already mentioned looking inward. Now add to that the idea of keeping it simple. It is easy to get overwhelmed. Heading straight to the minefield of our childhood and family for where most of our beliefs were either passed on or created isn't always the best approach. If you are not an experienced swimmer, enter the water slowly, see how it feels and get comfortable with the new experience.

I love the tool where a symptom or a circumstance can be used as information. As soon as you identify with depression, for instance, you *will* be depressed. On the other hand, if the sensation of depression has taken residence, what might it be telling you as far as where you have abandoned yourself? What does that mean? The beliefs that comprise your ego identity are no longer congruent with the needs and nurturing of your soul. That incongruence and lack of harmony within could be the source of depression.

Once you have this information, it's time for a little detective work. Investigation is an incredible tool that helps to unravel how the mind tends to automatically believe whatever it thinks. This can be an active process but usually a practice is required that gives some distance to our ego identity and the endless thinking it prefers. The Buddhists and others use meditation, some Christians use contemplative prayer, while the Sufis like to dance. Whatever works for you, silence and solitude are usually involved.

Keeping it simple, we can gain inner vision. Rather than identification with a symptom or circumstance, it can be taken as information into which the basic tools of investigation can be applied. This perspective might be called using your soul eyes. Modern culture would like us to believe that everything perceived through the five senses, along with our intellectual evaluation of that information, is the basis for our reality. Swallow the blue pill. The mystics through the ages have a different view. They say experiences of the external world are a *consequence* of our inner reality. The modern belief is that we have very little control over our lives. The soul view is that we have control to the extent that we want to take responsibility for our inner world. This is not to say that these realities are separate. For example, if I eat some junk food which causes me to feel ill, it's good information suggesting I might consider eating more nutritiously.

So, if you have gotten to the point where you can create some daily silence and solitude, what can now be done to change behaviors? Making a commitment to yourself that is in balance with your inner and outer life is a good beginning. There is also the conscious process to identify a false belief. For instance, deciding not to go to MacDonald's would be the result of no longer believing that any kind of caloric intake will do. A false belief can be quite subtle as well, especially if it is a shadow issue that is buried in the unconscious. Suffering is a wonderful gauge that shows something is awry. The world has just given you a low grade on one of its pop quizzes.

Keep pulling out the tools to create a reset and bring yourself back to who you really are. Some might call that your center or your loving. Self-forgiveness, meditation, yoga, prayer, contemplative practices, nature walks, deep breaths all allow for some distance from both our minds and the imposition of the external world. Through discipline and the practice of using these tools on a daily basis, a resilience is born which then creates the possibility of being more and more present with ourselves, in our relationships with others and with the world around us. Presence may be the greatest gift of all. That's what we are training for so when anything comes up, we're ready.

The Soul's Curriculum

The world of duality has been created from the view of the ego. This includes rich and poor, successful and unsuccessful, right and wrong along with good and bad at the top of a long, long list. Why from the ego? Because all of these ideas originate from the perspective of identity. In turn, all that we are seems to come from race, ethnicity, societal and religious beliefs, economic status, education, diet, even the clothes we wear and the vehicles we drive. Identity is simply what the ego creates to thrive and survive.

Out of this ego-centered world, a whole paradigm has been established that mimics the natural world in its potential for diversity. Where it diverges from the natural world is through the creation of fear-based beliefs. That fear focuses on the possibility of pain, suffering and ultimately, death. From this place, it is no wonder that worry, anxiety, depression and a general sense of never enough—personally and materially—have become the norm. This is reinforced in a capitalist culture that thrives on the concept that our own financial worth will never be ample. It can also be expanded beyond financial resources to our worth as humans—to ourselves, our families, communities and to the world. This capitalist idea is obsessed with success as an umbrella to validation, acceptance and approval.

Intermingled with the above is a learning system that promotes success over the origin of the word "education" which comes from the Latin word "educere" meaning to lead out or bring forth. Bring forth what? The old idea is that each one of us is instilled with some kind of genius as a gift of the soul. That genius wants to be discovered and nurtured so that it can help weave the fabric of the world. This gift is the essence of who we are. Our real work is to discover this essence. Happiness, peace of mind, contentment, whatever brings us joy is then found inside through that genius rather than outside with success or approval. The setup is quite clever. When joy is carried within, we don't have to rely on the external world to make us happy.

This option has always been available but perhaps less so today with the heavy hands of cultural indoctrination that keep the wheels of capitalism greased. As a result, a synthetic world has been created that is dominated by processed food, plastic, transient possessions, pollution, television laugh tracks, social media, chemical fertilizers and pesticides, artificial intelligence, screen time, mindless entertainment, robocalls and Western medicine that is wedded to pharmaceutical drugs and the quick fix of symptoms. For the most part, the world's culture has become one of instant gratification. This may be partly due to the mentality created through the use of technology. We seem to want to mimic the speed and efficiency of our modern devices. The shadow side is the loss of human attributes like common sense, civility, kindness, patience, intuition and self-reflection. In simpler terms, the seventeenth-century Japanese monk, Gensei, wrote, "The point in life is to know what's enough."

What has happened is the dominance of the ego-centered world in relation to the soul which has become practically an endangered species. In the broadest sense, the world's problems are the result of that ego-centered world believing that linear thinking, analysis and technology can provide all of the answers. Unfortunately, that hasn't worked out so well, as demonstrated by the destruction of the environment, climate change, racial inequality, economic and social injustice, nuclear proliferation and deadly viruses. From a soul-centered perspective, the ego is subservient to the needs of this deeper part of who we are. And since the soul originates from love, it has no interest in greed, lust, power, hate, anger or pride.

How does one discern between these two worlds? The Persian poet Rumi wrote, "Your task is not to seek for love, but merely to seek and find all the barriers within yourself that you have built against it." Fear beyond instinct and survival is something we learn. If it can be learned, it can be just as easily unlearned. Consider an acronym for fear—future events already realized. As an example, worry and anxiety are wonderful red flag warnings of being out of the present moment. Depression is another red flag indicating that one has lost sight of who they are. All emotions related to the fear-based world are further warnings of those barriers Rumi mentioned; the barriers we create to suppress the hidden love underneath, the love that exists within.

The soul makes no distinction between the good and the bad. It's all just experience that can be used as a gauge to discover what resonates personally and what doesn't. Learning this neutrality at some point is essential in creating some distance from the world of identity. Many religions use prayer or meditation as a way of reinforcing this point of view. It's in the silence that the soul can be experienced. Imagine getting in touch with a pure sense of peace inside, then carrying it out into the world for the rest of the day.

Buddhists believe that education should focus on training the mind to control the runaway train aspect of our thoughts. As the bumper sticker says, "Don't Believe Everything You Think." In tandem, training of the body needs to take place whether it be through exercise, diet, yoga or walking meditation. It's all training and it never needs to stop. Basically, there is a continual process of observing the world inside and around us, seeing what works, forgiving ourselves for what doesn't so that continual upgrading of our metaphorical operating system takes place for the duration of our physical lives. In other words, growing into our souls. That's the work.

To slightly alter a line from a Jack Gilbert poem, to make fear the only measure of your attention is to praise the devil. To make love the only measure, knowing that every experience (no matter how difficult) is here to grow our souls, then the world of possibilities becomes endless in the very light and breath that created the universe itself.

Where Do We Go From Here?

In Greek mythology, Nemesis was the Goddess of retribution giving punishment to those who were arrogant, had come into undeserved fortune or committed crimes with impunity. She restored balance in the world through justice. The modern version is that of an archrival. At the moment, the current pandemic is being viewed as the nemesis to our very survival. Often when we feel threatened, a war is then declared against the unknown including viruses, people or even through the subtle and overt ways that we are in conflict with nature herself. Sometimes the war works as with cholera and plague but oftentimes it doesn't, as with cancer, poverty and drugs.

The anthropologist Gregory Bateson said, "The major problems in the world are the result of the difference between how nature works and the way people think." How *does* nature work? Through cooperation (even in the midst of what appears to be chaos), adaptation and continually bringing itself into balance. The crises in the world are evidence of where we are no longer in harmony with nature and ourselves. With the melting of the ice caps, wildfires and record-breaking weather events, the result is the loss of over 150 species a day along with regular flooding from Venice to Miami. Add to this the failing of those institutions where we once put our faith. Anxiety, stress and depression have now become the norm.

The old paradigm is collapsing which seemed inevitable since it has become a runaway train going off the rails. That train carried unbridled economic growth producing more business and leisure travel, the resulting environmental harm, loss of personal and political civility and countless distractions provided by our electronic devices and entertainment. We have become a culture that no longer knows what it needs but only what it wants. Nature thrives through expansion which can only continue on for so long before it's time to go to seed, come to rest and then allow for the creation of new life.

I had been wondering recently how that old model of doing things might change and make way for something new. Along comes COVID-19 and the world has been quickly put on hold. Part of the train crashed through economics via the temporary downturn in the stock market and massive job loss. We have yet to see how it will rebound. Part is the reality of how those on the front lines will fare long-term in dealing with the sick and dying. While in the pause mode, another part is hopefully reconfiguring what the next step may be. The virus itself has no boundaries or discrimination which makes it a perfect parallel to our consumptive way of living. There is an old idea that the things which go wrong in our lives are here to help us. So blaming anything loses the opportunity for growth that a crisis presents. The challenge is not only with the physical but with the emotional, psychological and spiritual bodies.

Viruses need a host to survive so they're just looking for a home. Where do vagrants go? To the nearest abandoned building. Perhaps this disease is illustrating the extent to which we have abandoned ourselves and it has thus taken up residence accordingly? This is not to say that the precautions in place concerning social distancing, washing hands and general vigilance should be ignored. Prudence is in being attentive. But life is always asking us to go deeper. The Goddess Nemesis would offer humility as the cure to our arrogance as a species in relation to the rest of nature.

There is an old saying that anything we resist persists. Now that the pause is in place, hoping for the quick fix to go back to the previous lifestyle might be reconsidered. Keep the things that work but it's time to change the things that don't. What have any of us done personally to confront our anger, prejudices, griefs and inner wounds? This is part of the salve. Maybe the pandemic is trying to show us viscerally how interconnected we all are. Washing our hands of the things that no longer work is part of the mix. Placing a few boundaries around our seemingly unlimited desires would be a way to curtail the addictions that create our lives. Yes, take care of yourself and your body. But the less tangible antidote of taking us to a new future might be found through a deeper, authentic loving of ourselves and, in turn, of the world around us.

A Letter to a Friend

In case you were wondering, I thought I should elucidate my reasons for not being vaccinated at this time. There are several layers here so please bear with me.

First, my history with Western medicine has been an ongoing disaster. I've been lied to repeatedly (my favorite was that I was going deaf twenty years ago) by doctors. I was harmed and even threatened physically by an ear, nose and throat specialist when I was ten. At age twelve, my dentist told me that I was a "non-Novocainer." In other words, I have no history of good results with the exceptions of a great dentist in Colorado and my son's pediatrician.

My faith in Western medicine is limited to trauma care where, I believe, it is the best in the world, with a track record to back that up. It wasn't until I moved to New Mexico and began seeing a doctor of Oriental medicine that things changed drastically. I now visit him every other week and I think I may be in the best health and shape of my life. What a difference to see how allopathic medicine is focused on disease while Chinese medicine is focused on wellness. With the Western model, much responsibility is placed on the doctor to expediently fix whatever ails, either through surgery or pharmaceutical intervention. On the other hand, Chinese medicine puts its faith in the natural systems of the human body and uses only homeopathic remedies, acupuncture and body manipulation. Responsibility is placed on the individual rather than on external solutions.

You may already know that the United States represents a little over 4 percent of the world's population yet consumes 70 percent of the global pharmaceutical supply. Two out of every three Americans use a pharmaceutical drug at least once a month. Yes, we are a culture that is addicted to meds. Add illegal drug use and we are simply an addicted culture.

To drop down the pharmaceutical hole further, those companies spent $47.7 million in the first quarter of 2020 in lobbying Congress to make sure no generic versions of a vaccine would be allowed in the United States. Pfizer alone made a profit of three billion (yes, billion) dollars from its vaccine in the first quarter of this year. The good news is that they have sold two hundred million doses at no profit to the United States government for distribution around the world.

The bottom line for pharmaceutical companies is the bottom line, not health. They have so overtaken the medical profession that meds are considered as normal as breathing air. An interesting note is that those same companies have virtually no legal liability for the products they sell.

One thing that I know for sure is that there is no pharmaceutical drug made without side effects. That's just how it is when putting chemicals into a living organism. In terms of the three vaccines in use, they rely on biosynthetic material which is a very new technology in which no long-term studies exist. The idea of putting synthetic material in my bloodstream makes no sense to me. I'd just as soon eat genetically modified food. As one doctor in Vermont put it, the new vaccines represent the largest clinical study in the history of humans on this planet. A friend who used to run the ER here in Taos mirrored that same idea with, "We're all guinea pigs in this experiment."

I'm waiting patiently for a proven technology; that is, inactivated or attenuated vaccines to be allowed or developed in the United States. The idea that only three vaccines are available in a culture that insists on, even demands hundreds of television channels, styles of cars, clothing options, electronic devices, food choices, etc., is absurd. To me, it is outrageous to the extent that our government is in bed with the pharmaceutical industry thus severely limiting our choices for the benefit of Big Pharma's profit. Over one hundred vaccines are in development around the world with eight that have been approved for full use and nine for early or limited use here and elsewhere. Why haven't we seen any of those other fourteen? If our government wanted to end this pandemic sooner than later, every option should be available.

To consider even a broader picture, we live in a fear-based world. Western medicine thrives on that fear. It's the fear of suffering or dying which this culture rarely addresses. COVID-19 comes along and now dying is a more real possibility for about one in six hundred Americans.

I have lived in that fear-based world with it's nuclear proliferation; fights against everything from illicit drugs, cancer and heart disease; racism; prejudice; the increased purchase of guns by citizens in the past year; war; even the adversarial language used by our last president. But that world doesn't work because it's unsustainable which is the nature of fear itself. This is not to mention the very real effects of climate change that are upon us caused by our adversarial relationship to nature.

The alternative is something I've been trying to do for about the last fifteen years which is a love-based perspective of the world. How does that look? It's a radically different approach to life that puts full responsibility on the individual. So symptoms or viruses like COVID become information rather than something to be immediately banished (for the sake of someone's profit). Or if my world turns upside down, I first have to look inside rather than resort to shame or blame.

One hundred percent responsibility is not taught in our schools or universities. And this is not to say that I have any problem with someone who chooses to get the current vaccines. Most of my friends and all of my family have. I support their decisions and feel that it is not my business to tell someone how to live their life. Making it my business is a symptom of the fear-based world and a sure path to suffering.

So what has COVID-19 been trying to tell us? To me, it's how we have abandoned ourselves, our health, our caring and our relationship to the natural world for the sake of expediency and a lifestyle. We've become perfect reflections of the technological world in our desire for speed and efficiency at the expense of caring and connection. I've been feeling this in the past month with the onslaught of tourist traffic, too few employees to deal with those tourists and a general feeling that we need to get right back to where we were before the pandemic. Well, that world was hardly functioning very well to begin with. It's all too much and too soon. Did anyone self-reflect in the past eighteen months?

One of the side effects already at hand is the kind of non-vaccinated shaming I've experienced from friends who are living in that fear-based world, who are stuck in their heads or both. Yes, they are afraid of losing their lifestyles and want me to support them on their path of attachment. I listen patiently but am not interested in that world of suffering. The reality is that I live in somewhat of a bubble with human interaction mostly at the gym where I swim and at the grocery store. Yes, I still wear a mask in public which is my responsibility. I have great faith in my prudence, my commitment to a healthy body (I swim seven hours a week and hike about another three to six), eat only healthy foods and try to live my own curriculum. And I'm not afraid of death. I'd rather die knowing that I did my best in living the life my soul wanted versus abandoning myself for the sake of a paradigm that is collapsing.

We'll get through this pandemic. We did one hundred years ago without vaccines. Some will die along the way but that is exactly how nature works. To fight against the way of the natural world is the height of human arrogance.

Mortality

The saddest moment of my childhood had nothing to do with losing a toy, a pet or a friend. In retrospect, I can even tell you the date when this happened: October 9, 1956. It was my last day as a four-year-old. I can clearly remember sitting on a two-foot-high stone curb next to our driveway, hands under my elbows, leaning forward on my thighs. I was thinking about how I was turning a corner from the lightness of being young to the weight of becoming older. Such strange ponderings for a four-year-old. Of course, those thoughts vanished during the subsequent birthday festivities and the accompanying sugar rush. The spell of youth lasts until the first sudden heartbreak or realization.

That weight has always dogged me, though it would be temporarily overcome by the confusion of wondering if I was in the right family and the anxiety of not knowing how to even be in the world throughout my teen years. Thank God for the folk music movement and the surety of holding a guitar in my hands. Two grandparents died during this time but there were never any discussions about their passing and no funerals to attend. College kept the family denial around death at arm's length. I went to a school six hours away but I still floundered. Just after graduation, a friend at that school committed suicide by hanging. This was well after Jimi Hendrix, Janis Joplin and Jim Morrison died but the first near encounter with death in my adult body.

Then my closer musical heroes and heroines began to disappear, including Tim Buckley and Sandy Denny. Her song "Who Knows Where The Time Goes" became an anthem for that weight I carried within me. I remember once seeing Linda Ronstadt in her prime at the Saratoga Performing Arts Center and how her voice wrapped around my body leaving me with the anchor and certainty of beauty. Now she can no longer sing due to Parkinson's disease. During college, my first foray as a musician into electric music was playing rhythm guitar and singing in a blues band. My assignment was to learn every song off Paul Butterfield's first two albums. This was electric blues at its best. One song, "Born In Chicago" has a last verse that has stayed with me all these years later.

> *Well, now rules are alright if there's someone left to play the game*
>
> *All my friends are going and things just don't seem the same.*

The blues was always there in folk music but something different was getting expressed when it became electric. Once the guitar became amplified, a new door (albeit a back door) opened to the heart. When Albert King sang about lost love, I was thrown into a whole new world.

I'm gonna leave it up to you, so long, girl, so long good bye

My love will follow you, as the years go passing by.

Friends and lovers come and go but the love created never dies—which feels like a universal truth to be reconciled personally or maybe not at all. If it could be figured out easily and clearly, then it wouldn't be soulful, would it?

In the film *The Seventh Seal,* Ingmar Bergman confronted this conundrum existentially between his main character—a knight coming home from the Crusades—and a personification of Death. The two make a deal that the knight's life will be spared for the duration of a chess match played between them. This extra time is spent by the knight trying to discover if God exists or not. Watching this in college took me right into an abyss since spirituality was absent during my childhood. It was complicated enough to *feel* the loss of someone but adding the dimension of the possible presence of God, or not, was overwhelming. From there one could get lost in questions of free will, fate, destiny and any purpose to being alive. Now, more weight was being added.

During my middle years, there was the occasional loss through cancer, a car accident or old age. When my father died nine years ago, it changed my landscape forever. It was time but he did something I never expected. The decisions throughout his life were always made with either his father or his wife, my mother. Always. In the last months, he had a heart event that left him in a coma. When it came to the time of his passing, he did it alone which I couldn't have imagined. Larry Levis writes about this in his poem "The City of Light."

The last thing my father did for me
Was map a way: he died, & so
Made death possible. If he could do it, I
Will also, someday, be so honored

Since his death, the procession has begun in earnest: another friend from college, friends where I live, poets, more musicians and Bergman himself. The circle keeps turning as I watch my contemporaries with their bodies falling apart or succumbing to the results of long-term bad habits. In response, I'm still dancing, swimming laps, hiking and doing as much as I can to take care of myself.

I dreamt recently of a Great Blue Heron flying out of nowhere, landing on my back and just staying there like a form of protection. It was the color of the Pacific Ocean—deep blue and vibrant. Even with the ongoing quiet parade of losses and my own attempt at coming to terms with the inevitable, I know that I am blessed. Oh, the things I could have told my younger self from this perspective. But why ruin the ride?

Luminescence of the Ordinary

There is an enduring theme in art of being given a second chance, often after a certain amount of pleading or being transformed through realization. The stakes are raised when the chance is a return to Earth from heaven like what happened to Joe Pendleton in the film *Here Comes Mr. Jordan* (or in the remake *Heaven Can Wait* with Warren Beatty). Another variation on this idea of a second chance is death as a potential found in Dicken's *A Christmas Carol* and illustrated by George Bailey's character in *It's A Wonderful Life*. For Scrooge and Bailey, there are only two choices—change or die.

In *Here Comes Mr Jordan*, Pendleton rightly complains that his time is not up. It turns out that there was a mistake so back to Earth he goes. Scrooge is faced with a moral dilemma by confronting whether he will get in touch with his humanity or not. Bailey must come to terms with what his guardian angel, Clarence, has told him: "Strange, isn't it? Each man's life touches so many other lives, and when he isn't around he leaves an awful hole, doesn't he?" Scrooge got to see the past, present and future as a way of seeking redemption. The update to that theme was Bailey's witnessing the same time span *without* his presence which was enough to turn things around.

I was in high school when I first really thought about death and the accompanying fear that the world would continue on without my presence. This was an existential crisis that lingered until it expressed itself as full blown physical experiences through several panic attacks I had at the end of my marriage years ago. One night I woke up to the utter certainty that I was in a coffin and would never get to see my young son again. No pleading or negotiation was possible but just the finality of being dead and separated from the living. I began therapy thanks to those attacks. Since then, it's been a long process of learning to manage my fears.

Leaping forward past my marriage and my career, my view of second chances has altered slightly from the examples mentioned above. I have a personal variation which has made living that much more precious by imagining dying and going to the other side. There I plead with the divine to just give me twenty-four hours back on Earth because I miss it so much. I'm referring to everything in nature along with laughing with a friend, being touched by a lover, hearing music (I'd immediately pick "Tekere" by Salif Kieta), tasting Thai food, dancing, swimming, smelling plumeria once again or just hearing my mother's voice. Sometimes when we are talking on the phone, a feeling will come over me of how incredibly lucky I am to still have a parent alive to speak to. I'll cry silently, not wanting to interrupt the conversation, while being drenched in the gratitude of that sensation.

This thankfulness and appreciation began years ago in the West Indies while anchored in the bay between Gros and Petite Piton (volcanic plugs that rise quickly) off the island of St. Lucia. It had been two days of traveling from home to finally get on a boat and sail. The seas were calm, the winds steady and it was heaven to feel warm tropical breezes on my skin. Getting that far took most of the day so when dinner was done, the sky had become a burst of stars down to the surface of the water. As I was rinsing a rag off the stern of the boat, phosphorescence illuminated in the stirred-up ocean. Everywhere I looked there were sparks of light scattered across the sea and the sky. I was awestruck in the first-hand knowledge of the presence of far greater energies than myself.

That feeling now happens a few times a year usually without advance notice. Often, but not always, it's prompted by a piece of music. When the music is live, like one time dancing to a kora (West African stringed harp), there is barely a separation between the musician's played notes and my body's response to the rhythm and texture of those sounds. This immediacy, or presence, is a continual reminder of what it is to be truly alive. Thank God for live music.

When I'm playing and singing a song on my own, there are moments of being transported to some place that feels enchanted, a kind of spell, like I've become the song itself. Then I'll finish the tune and have no idea how the music just happened. I'll only know that it felt great.

Recently, I was running some errands locally and on the way home, a particular piece of music ("The Way Up," Part 4) by The Pat Metheny Group came out of the car CD player that I hadn't heard in some time. There is a simple repeating guitar line in the second part of this section which is trance-like. The road where I was driving had gentle curves as it winds through horse and cow pastures. Spring was in the air, bringing that virgin green color to the grass, the fields and the newly blossoming trees. All of this was in contrast to a New Mexican blue sky partially filled with morning clouds. If you had filmed this moment, you'd see that there was nothing out of the ordinary taking place. But that feeling of coming from the other side just to experience the simple ordinary pleasures of being alive arrived like a Pacific wave to take me for a ride. With that came a deep cherishing of my own breath, the wind in my hair, that smell of newness, music (MUSIC!!) in my ears, the sky, the clouds, the road—everything utterly ordinary yet so dear that I wanted to caress it like the first time I ever held my newly born son in my arms. Yes, to experience the world as if brand new but with the adult knowledge of its fleeting preciousness. Tears.

Just give me twenty-four more hours.

A Blessing

Autumn's fallen leaves held fast under a few inches of snow as I walked up a favorite trail to tend cairns and find relief after two weeks of loss after loss, leaving little to hold on to except a belief that nature might provide some kind of solace, even refuge. Tony Hoagland, a poet acquaintance, sadly succumbed to cancer. Roy Hargrove, jazz musician a generation younger than me, had a cardiac arrest after kidney failure. Innocents were gunned down in a synagogue, convenience store and yoga studio. And paradoxically, there has been political spending on ads that could easily have bought homes for all migrant caravan families walking the length of Mexico.

Short days, long shadows and an unfamiliar companion feeling of apprehension held me as I walked on, wondering if it was fear or, more specifically, if even being with the trees, the creek and the silence was no longer safe. Up this particular trail there is an aspen grove, like a cathedral, that longs for the sky while the tree roots weave a party-line fabric. It's one closely knit family talking to each other about weather and seasonal changes. Out of the grove, the trail opens up again so one can see across a creek to a steep hillside held together mostly by pines, their boughs recently covered in snow and like the aspens, combing the deep blue New Mexican sky for windswept messages telling of possible endings to the drought.

All of a sudden, the silence was fractured by the sound of breaking branches—a commotion by something large, maybe dangerous. My apprehension rose to attention but not enough to run, being aware of the ravine and a creek between the noise and me. Still time to react if necessary. In a second, I turned and out of the pines rose a bird in shades of brown arrowing at an angle, breaking through the trees. Then it turned slightly, giving me a full view of a six-foot wingspan. Did I just see a Golden Eagle? Swiftly, gone.

Earlier in the summer, there was a juvenile rattlesnake in the kitchen and a newborn of the same species in the compost, followed by dreams of them both. Last night, I dreamt of tide pools in Kealakekua Bay (like the glorious ones in Kapoho recently covered by lava) on the Big Island with students everywhere, studying the coral. My understanding of things can be so slow—from seconds to years later, if at all. How I long to be that eagle, bursting out of the thick, navigating every hindrance, soaring towards the freedom of the sky, bold as love.

Towards a New Paradigm

It was announced recently that the Boy Scouts of America declared bankruptcy due to legal costs "to create a trust to provide compensation for victims" (NPR). The places where we used to put our faith are collapsing one after another. Included are religion and some of its clergy, government, politicians, education, traditional marriage, the ethics of some doctors, finance, safety in our schools, civility and common sense. Even the strides of Western medicine have created a shadow with the overprescribing of pharmaceutical drugs and the ensuing consequences of addiction. Intertwined with all of this are the unfolding environmental catastrophes from species extinction to unpredictable weather events to the melting of the ice caps and the pollution of the oceans. Some might say that it is the end of the world. If nothing else, the catastrophic consequences of business as usual are at hand.

These examples are symptomatic of human behavior that has gone awry. In "The Second Coming," William Butler Yeats wrote, "Things fall apart; the centre cannot hold." That was first published in 1920, over one hundred years ago. Since humans have had such a pervasive impact on the planet, our very survival as a species is no longer guaranteed. The Bulletin of Atomic Scientists has put the doomsday clock at one hundred seconds to midnight—closer than ever before. The proliferation of nuclear weapons in the hands of unstable leaders and the climate crises are major factors in our impending demise. Despair is very real at this moment in time. When "the centre cannot hold," finding faith in solutions can be elusive.

Albert Einstein once said, "We can't solve problems by using the same kind of thinking we used when we created them." This implies that the standard view of realty needs to be reevaluated. That view assumed that all things are separate, that humans can exploit and destroy each other along with other species. That we can pollute the earth with no thought as to consequences and that the way of nature is inferior to the thinking of man. This is the ego-centered world that appears to be doing itself in—albeit unconsciously. How does one find a way in times like these?

Individual reality is based on our genetic makeup, environmental factors, family backgrounds and individual beliefs—all of which create the lens for how we view being alive (and/or dying). This is the basic setup. Beyond the basic, science tells us that 95 percent of our greater awareness is in the unconscious. If you believe that the universe is based on unconditional love which responds to everything accordingly, then our unconscious is attracting whatever people and circumstances that are ideal for our individual growth and development. If one adopts this view that reality, as a consequence of divine loving, has tailor-made our lives for the potential evolution of our souls, then shame and blame are no longer possible. Out goes the old, yet current, model. But what is the new? Without shaming or blaming others or God for what's going wrong, there's the possibility of taking *total* responsibility for everything in our lives. This may sound like a leap but if you accept the first premise that we are somehow attracting everything that happens to us, consciously or not, then taking full responsibility for our lives is the next step.

This is not to say that I might be the cause of cancer in others. What it does say is that I can use the situation to look within to see where I no longer know who I am as far as benefiting myself and the world around me. The Indian philosopher Krishnamurti wrote, "War is the spectacular and bloody projection of our everyday living." In other words, until each one of us can find inner peace, war will continue. So if I am worrying about the environmental crisis at hand, the first step is for me to take a close look at my own carbon footprint. What is my contribution to the problem? Beyond that, where do I allow polluting thoughts to enter my consciousness? Where have I sullied a relationship with my unresolved anger or grief? Or where have I trashed my creativity, my loving and my life?

The physical, emotional and psychological processes and work are good but can be consuming if done exclusively. With so many things entering our field of awareness all of the time, other tools are needed to deal with the onslaught of everyday life. One of the advocates of taking 100 percent responsibility is Dr. Hew Len who has brought the Hawaiian spiritual practice of ho'oponopono (to make right, to bring into balance) forward. This forgiveness work includes saying silently to oneself, "I'm sorry, forgive me, thank you, I love you" whenever anything comes up. The expanded version of this is "I'm sorry" for anything I, my family, my ancestors or my genetic line may have done to create this situation. "Forgive me" for any part I, or they, may have played. "Thank you" for bringing this up so I can clean it and "I love you" to yourself to eliminate any possibility of personal blame or shame.

What we are doing through forgiveness, meditation or any practice that brings us back to our center and our loving is resetting energy internally. That reset is just like a pebble thrown in a pond creating ripples that amplify the original splash in all directions. Another way to approach this idea of total responsibility is by discerning if our actions are in favor of or against some situation, person or circumstance. The best resilience is finding inner peace first and foremost. The ultimate test is whether an action or thought is coming from love or not.

Living during this time provides us with the easy and obvious identification of where and how the old way is failing. The repercussions are everywhere. But don't be fooled. The old reference points of acceptance, approval, validation, shame, blame, identity, success, fame and power still prevail. As these trends continue to usurp the principles and values that once created strength in our institutions, we witness the collapse. A new paradigm still to be defined makes our individual inner work more important than ever. After all of the years of external focus, it's time to get back to our souls and the inherent loving found there. Rather than forward motion, let's try going inward and seeing what grace can provide.

Since The Vaccine

Since the vaccine, government actually works, science makes a comeback!

Since the vaccine, anti-vaxxers said that my left eyeball would fall out. Instead, the middle finger on my right hand no longer bends and keeps pointing towards the sky.

Since the vaccine, QAnon reveals that overwhelming numbers of unvaccinated feral cats are the real cause of voter fraud. Fourteen states outlaw voting in any pet adoption locations.

Since the vaccine, Washington has gone from dysfunctionally to functionally gridlocked.

Since the vaccine, talks are underway to reunite the Dakotas, Carolinas, Californias and maybe even the Americas.

Since the vaccine, Europe got even older.

Since the vaccine, the National Parks are now as popular as sexting. Remember, take only pictures, leave only digital footprints.

Since the vaccine, Jeff Bezos will pay to vaccinate the rest of the world—but only after we become Amazon Prime members.

Since the vaccine, the Kardashian's television run has ended. Coincidence or what?

Since the vaccine, Hollywood blockbusters and contrails return. Did anyone really miss them?

Since the vaccine, there's no business like the pharmaceutical business.

Since the vaccine, "modified" no longer exclusively applies to behavior.

Since the vaccine, modern medicine forestalls the end of the world!

Since the vaccine, unsubstantiated research says that I'll live long enough to witness the next pandemic.

Since the vaccine, thank God the toilet paper cartel was finally busted.

Since the vaccine, living on the edge is fondly remembered through empty roads and take-out that felt just like the old days of scoring drugs.

Since the vaccine, nostalgia is creeping in for the minimization of small talk thanks to face masks.

Since the vaccine, we find out who our real friends are.

Since the vaccine and thanks to 5G, I can now text telepathically.

Since the vaccine, my son has become the paintball warlord his computer games predicted.

Since the vaccine, my girlfriend says our love-making is now off the Richter scale. Looking forward to that booster shot.

Since the vaccine, reading is a challenge with only one eyeball working.

Since the vaccine, I can't find my monocle.

Since the vaccine, tax credits for body parts that have fallen off!

Since the vaccine, new appreciation for those parts still hanging on.

Since the vaccine, I praise chlorine(!) for helping to keep me safe in my local swimming pool.

Since the vaccine, dancing to live music is still cool.

Since the vaccine, the summer of redemption never happened.

Since the vaccine, the sobering reality is that viruses never really go away.

Since the vaccine, Jacinda Ardern for President of the newly created Earth Federation.

Since the vaccine, my girlfriend rocks!

Since the vaccine, back to normal actually means forward to abnormal.

Since the vaccine, what's the freakin' rush?

Everything Explained

Birth—Transformation from relative obscurity to starring in the role of a lifetime.

Sex—*Way* more fun than birth, childhood and initiation combined.

Education—Without teaching "the birds and the bees," filling the void with conspiracy theories about how babies are made. Yo stork!

Conspiracy Theories—Facts are for sissies.

Gravity—The opposite of a conspiracy theory unless you believe in "the Rapture."

"The Rapture"—Sex for most but for some Christians the belief that God will "friend" you on Facebook.

Facebook—The modern equivalent of going to the drive-in by keeping your "friends" at a comfortable distance while staring at a screen.

Drive-ins—Who knew that they'd be so far ahead of their time? Except for the Rapture part which is timeless!

Face Masks—According to "freedom" lovers, a muzzling device to silence "fake news" about the existence of pandemics and the law of gravity. Not required at the drive-in.

Fake News—"Satan's Skull Found In New Mexico," *Weekly World News*, March 13, 1993.

New Mexico—From aliens, acequias, art and the atomic bomb, it's first in diversity.

Diversity—Both the cause and solution to America's problems. Evidence that mimicking nature actually works!

Evidence—A good thing to have if you are going to court to try and prove a conspiracy theory.

Court—Where a legal proceeding takes place to question witnesses or a way to get to some of that Rapture.

Question—A thought process currently in lockdown. Does an app work instead?

Work—What the Federal minimum wage hasn't done in years.

Wage—Betting that the KGB collects data from conspiracy theorists' social media accounts for potential recruitment.

The Deep State—QAnon believers recruited as KGB operatives.

Social Media—A diversion from reality when you should be wondering if you have enough toilet paper to last through a quarantine.

Quarantine—An alternate way of saying that we screwed up, got busted and were convicted.

Conviction—Thanks to all of the women of the world, it's how we got here.

Women—One of two or more sexes, but who's counting?

Counting—On a break from the last four years watching the reality show version of *The Godfather* morphing into *Apocalypse Now*

Knowledge—Allegedly anything that is posted on social media.

Wisdom—Having enough sanitizer and face masks for the long haul.

Intuition—The gut feeling that "the Rapture" may just be a metaphor.

Metaphor—A figure of speech that is symbolic rather than literal, often used in poetry... now I've lost you.

Taking A Break—Shutting off all screens and for just a moment bathing in the silence and solitude that this downtime affords. Especially if your kids and partner are driving you nuts.

Relationships—The real education.

Parenting—Sometimes a form of initiation, oftentimes not. But definitely a deep state.

Grandparenting—Another form of rapture.

Death—Even after a whole lifetime of work, no experience necessary.

The Secret of Life—Babies.

A New Declaration of Independence

The unanimous Declaration of the fifty United States of America, When in the course of human events, it becomes necessary for one people to dissolve the oppressions that have connected them as a nation, and to assume among the powers of the earth, the separate and equal station to which the Laws of Nature and the Divine entitle them, a decent respect to the opinions of humanity requires that they should declare the causes that impel them to the relief of those oppressions.

We hold these truths to be self-evident, that all people are created equal regardless of gender, race or color, that they are endowed by their Creator with certain unalienable rights, that among these are Life, Liberty and the pursuit of Peace and Happiness.—To ensure these tenets, Governments are instituted among people, deriving their just powers from the consent of the governed,—That whenever any form of Government becomes destructive of these ends, it is the Right of the People to alter or to abolish it, and to institute new just Government that provides for the well-being of all, laying its foundation on such principles and organizing its powers in such form, as to them shall seem most likely to effect their Safety and Security. Prudence, indeed, will dictate that Governments long established should not be changed for light and transient causes; and accordingly all experience hath shown, that humans are more disposed to suffer, while evils are sufferable, than to right themselves by abolishing the forms to which they are accustomed. But when a long train of abuses and usurpations, pursuing invariably the same object evinces a design to reduce them under outdated beliefs, it is their right, it is their duty, to throw off such Government, and to provide new Guards for their future security. Such has been the patient sufferance of these States; and such is now the necessity that constrains them to alter their former Systems of Government. The history of the old paradigm is a history of repeated injuries and usurpations, all having in direct object the establishment of an unsustainable way of living over and within these States. To this end, we propose a new paradigm using the Constitution of the United States as a beginning rather than an end to which revisions are long overdue. To prove this, let Facts be submitted to a candid world.

> The Electoral College is hereby abolished allowing for a simple majority vote to decide the outcome of Presidential elections.
>
> The Citizens United decision by the Supreme Court will hereby be vacated thus removing, in this instance, the undue influence of money over politics. All financial contributions to politicians and politi-

cal campaigns will be strictly limited to twenty-five dollars per person per election or campaign. Corporations and other nonhuman entities are forbidden to participate.

Lobbying of any form to further the undue influence of money will hereby be prohibited.

Rather than two major political parties, multiple groups shall be encouraged to represent more than one perspective of economic and social beliefs. Thus, without the singular focus of keeping capitalism alive regardless of threat to the environment and its citizens, a more perfect union may be possible.

Defense spending shall hereby be curtailed to account for no more than 10 percent of the national budget. Any available funds shall be used to help transition to the new paradigm through retraining towards sustainable energy sources; social programs that help veterans, the incarcerated, addicts, youth and the disenfranchised; a renaissance of diverse farming that promotes regenerative life and crop diversity; the establishment of universal healthcare; and an educational system that is soul-based rather than one focused on indoctrination.

A Department of Peace shall be formed along with a volunteer corps that utilizes the talents of the elderly, veterans, previously incarcerated, youth and all those who want to promote peace as a value that takes priority over violence.

The Environmental Protection Agency shall henceforth become a cabinet level department with full authority and responsibility to ensure the well-being of the planet and all its ecosystems, including waters, air, soils and every life-form within our purview.

The United States Postal Service shall be fully funded to particularly meet the needs of future elections conducted by mail.

The funding for public radio and television shall be restored in tandem with the breakup of the media giants so that unbiased and diverse information shall be the norm rather than the exception. In turn, the societal dependance on digital information and social networks shall be discouraged in order to promote imagination and creativity.

The members of the Supreme and Circuit Courts shall come under review every ten years providing for possible removal should it be determined that an agenda other than jurisprudence has become evident.

All statues, monuments, street signs and any remembrance of the United State's history of oppression shall be placed in museums to remind us of a past that need not be repeated.

The criminal justice system shall be reformed so that the possibility of rehabilitation takes precedence over punishment. The death penalty is hereby abolished.

Juneteenth shall hereby become a National Holiday also known as "Amends Day" to honor, by asking forgiveness, silently or otherwise, from all of those who have been enslaved, oppressed or mistreated by anyone who has felt superior to another.

A new National Anthem shall be commissioned based on the call of and feeling for the land rather than the fight to dominate it.

Daylight Savings Time is hereby rescinded.

Roadside billboards shall be removed and prohibited so that the landscape is no longer obscured.

As in nature, diversity shall be promoted through citizenry. Equally, citizens are encouraged to keep in touch with nature to be reminded of diversity and adaptation in the natural world along with the concept of when and what is enough. As the Divine's creation, the template of nature shall serve as both the guide and light to our new future.

America has become a culture based on corporate power, arrogance, fear and complacency with communications and news sources limited to a handful of corporate venues. Instead, democracy at its broadest should form a governance that reflects love, tolerance, compassion and caring not only for fellow humans but for the earth, its environment and all of its inhabitants. Of primacy would be the reversal of climate change to ensure the continuation of biological diversity upon our planet as well as the human race.

We, therefore, the people of the United States of

America, appealing to the Supreme Judge of the world for the rectitude of our intentions, do, in the Name, and by Authority of the good People of these States, solemnly publish and declare a new paradigm that excludes no one and promotes peace, justice and the possibility of one nation, indivisible, committed to compassion and the well-being of all of its inhabitants. And for the support of this Declaration, with a firm reliance on the protection of divine Providence, we mutually pledge to each other our Lives, our Fortunes and our sacred Honor.

My Prayer

May I be happy, may I have the ease of well-being.

May I be mentally, physically, emotionally and spiritually well.

I forgive myself for believing (or judging)...

May my son be well, may my mother be well, may my father be in peace.

May all those who have gone before be well and in peace.

May my older brother and his family be well. May my older sister and her family be well.

May my younger brother and his family be well.

May my aunt and her family be well.

May my nieces, nephews, cousins and all of their families be well.

May my friends, acquaintances and all of their families be well.

May the whole world be well and in peace.

May I heal. May those who are near to me heal.

May all those who are crossing over be in peace.

For those who are suffering, may there be some relief to their pain.

May all of the women I know who are wanting healing, be healed.

May all of the women I know who have cancer be free of cancer.

May all of the men I know who are wanting to be healed, be healed.

May all of the men I know who have cancer be freeof cancer.

May all those who desire healing find the courage, strength, love, compassion, self-forgiveness and support that they need in order to make it happen.

May the living love that pours from my heart wrap around all living things and creatures above, below and on the surface of the earth. May it surround the earth itself and extend throughout the heavens and beyond.

May I be free of shame, blame, judgment and attachment.

May I be filled with love, happiness, grace and humility.

May I be safe and free from danger.

May I be filled with equanimity, joy, loving kindness, compassion and gratitude.

May the world be filled with equanimity, joy, loving kindness, compassion and gratitude.

May there be peace, love, and light everywhere.

Angels, guides, teachers, beings of light, all those who are watching over me, may I find grace.

Light switch on. This is a ho'oponopono practice that brings energy to whatever. For instance, "light switch on the healing of the planet." I do a whole list here with whatever is happening in my life at the moment. Then I finish up with:

Light switch on healing, recovery and reconciliation in the world.

Light switch on peace, love and light throughout the world.

Light switch on the whole wide world.

Thank you for my gifts, talents, blessings, and abundance.

Thank you for the gift of this life.

Amen

www.ingramcontent.com/pod-product-compliance
Lightning Source LLC
Chambersburg PA
CBHW070426010526
44118CB00014B/1927